DO YOU LIKE FOOTBALL?

If you do, this book is for you. Football has a rich tradition full of great moments, incredible players, and awesome teams. These are their tales—some from the past, some as fresh as last season! Along with the highlights, you'll be treated to photographs straight from *Sports Illustrated* that make you feel as if you're there on the field and a part of the action. *Sports Illustrated* is known for its coverage of the finest moments in sports. Now, here are those moments—just waiting for you!

Books by Bill Gutman

Sports Illustrated/BASEBALL'S RECORD BREAKERS
Sports Illustrated/GREAT MOMENTS IN BASEBALL
Sports Illustrated/GREAT MOMENTS IN PRO FOOTBALL
Sports Illustrated/PRO FOOTBALL'S RECORD BREAKERS
Sports Illustrated/STRANGE AND AMAZING BASEBALL
    STORIES
Sports Illustrated/STRANGE AND AMAZING FOOTBALL
    STORIES
BASEBALL'S HOT NEW STARS
GREAT SPORTS UPSETS
REFRIGERATOR PERRY
STRANGE AND AMAZING WRESTLING STORIES

Available from ARCHWAY Paperbacks

Sports Illustrated

GREAT MOMENTS
IN PRO FOOTBALL

Bill Gutman

AN ARCHWAY PAPERBACK
Published by POCKET BOOKS
New York   London   Toronto   Sydney   Tokyo

Photographs courtesy of *Sports Illustrated:* Sheedy & Long:
pp. 9, 13: Arthur Shay: p. 28; Neil Leifer: pp. 40, 77; James
Drake: p. 41; Heinz Kluetmeier: pp. 46, 99, 105; Rich Clarkson:
p. 49; John Iacono: p. 55; Walter Iooss Jr.: pp. 61, 85, 93, 115;
Jerry Cooke: p. 67; Richard Mackson: p. 70; Ronald C. Modra:
p. 107; Peter Read Miller: p. 117; John Biever: p. 119.

AN ARCHWAY PAPERBACK *Original*

An Archway Paperback published by
POCKET BOOKS, a division of Simon & Schuster Inc.
1230 Avenue of the Americas, New York, NY 10020

ISBN: 0-671-63015-6

First Archway Paperback printing September 1986

10 9 8 7 6 5 4

Printed in the U.S.A.

Contents

*The Galloping Ghost
Runs Wild*

His nickname was perhaps the most famous in football history—the Galloping Ghost. It conjured up images of power, speed, and elusiveness. When Harold "Red" Grange played for the University of Illinois in the mid-1920s, his gridiron exploits and his nickname became news headlines.

He could have easily been the inspiration for the phrase "a legend in his own time," because Red Grange was certainly that and a lot more. By the time he began his final season at Illinois in the fall of 1925, the Galloping Ghost was undoubtedly one of the best known and most highly visible athletes in the country.

His reputation was made on Saturday afternoons, when he did his thing on the gridiron like no other man of his time. In fact, it was a particular Saturday in 1924 when Red Grange cemented his place in football his-

1

tory forever. It was October 18, and the fighting Illini were meeting the Wolverines of Michigan in a Big Ten showdown.

The game might have been a hard-fought contest had it not been for the presence of Red Grange. For on this day the Galloping Ghost took a football game and turned it into a virtuoso performance perhaps unmatched in the annals of the gridiron sport. For the more than 67,000 fans who witnessed the spectacle, Red Grange must have indeed appeared to be a ghost, an elusive figure who was operating on a wholly different level than everyone else, the mere mortals.

Grange didn't waste any time getting started. He took the opening kickoff on his own five-yard line and bolted upfield. Weaving his way through the Michigan defenders, he took the ball back 95 yards for a touchdown. And the game was not yet ten seconds old!

But that was just the beginning. On the next Illinois drive, he got the ball again and immediately showed how much he hated being tackled. He weaved and dodged, cut and sprinted, and finally crossed the goal line, 66 yards downfield from the line of scrimmage. Minutes later, with the Wolverines still trying to determine what had hit them, Grange gave an encore performance. This time it was from 56 yards out, and once again the Michigan tacklers were left sprawling all over the gridiron.

How could they stop this human lightning bolt? The Michigan coaches tried to adjust their defenses, but the next time Illinois got the ball, it happened all over again. Grange took a handoff and was through the Michigan line like a shot. Once in the secondary, he worked his magic once more, this time speeding 43 yards for his fourth touchdown of the day. And even more amazing was the fact that the "day" was not yet 12 minutes old.

With the game all but over in those first minutes of the opening period, Grange played sparingly the rest of the way. But he did return to run thirteen yards for a score in the third period and then to throw an 18-yard touchdown pass in the fourth. When the day ended, he had scored five touchdowns and had amassed an amazing 402 yards in total offense!

It was a great moment never to be forgotten. The redhead had other great days, such as when he galloped for 363 yards on 36 carries against the University of Pennsylvania the following season. That game was played on a field so wet and muddy that it often looked like quicksand. But while most of the other players sloshed around as if they were in neutral, Red Grange glided, often untouched, making brilliant run after brilliant run.

But it was really those first twelve minutes against Michigan that captured the essence of the man. After his college career ended, Red Grange became the most marketed athlete of his time—or maybe any time. Even the pros bent to accommodate the man they hoped would put a young National Football League on the map. Grange signed with the Chicago Bears immediately upon completion of his senior season at Illinois, and the Bears arranged a special exhibition schedule that lasted until the end of January, just to showcase their newest player.

With the big, tough pros gunning for him, and weakened by a hectic schedule and extended season, Grange took a brutal battering. Today they might call it burnout. Or maybe there was no way any man could have lived up to the advance billing given Red Grange.

Whatever it was, his pro career was a disappointment. Red Grange never again reached the heights he had achieved as a collegian. By 1926 he and his manager, C. C. Pyle, broke with the Bears and tried to start their own league. That venture also failed.

Finally the Galloping Ghost did return to the Bears, but he never became a great pro runner. He spent his final six seasons in Chicago mainly as an above average *defensive back,* playing in the relative anonymity of the Bears' defensive backfield.

But none of that could ever diminish his achievements at Illinois, especially the unbelievable moment he had produced on a cold October afternoon in 1924. For that day Red Grange was perhaps the most superb football player who ever lived.

Say Hello to the Alabama Antelope

There probably isn't a pro football player alive who doesn't remember his first game as a pro. Whether it was good or bad, a player's first game is definitely a moment to remember.

One player who has the fondest of memories is the incomparable Alabama Antelope, Don Hutson, one of the greatest wide receivers ever to play the game. He created a great moment the very first time he stepped on an NFL gridiron. But unlike some other players who have debuted with flash and then faded, Hutson continued to produce great moments throughout his long career.

He came out of the University of Alabama as a tall, thin, but fast wide receiver who had helped lead the Crimson Tide to a Rose Bowl victory over Stanford on January 1, 1935, by catching six passes for 165 yards and two scores. It capped a great college career, but many pro football people wondered if Hutson was rugged enough for the pro game. They also questioned whether his style of play, full of fakes and fancy footwork, was suited for the NFL, whose offenses, at that time, did not depend on passing.

One NFL coach who wanted the thin receiver was Curly Lambeau of the Green Bay Packers. He had seen Hutson play at Alabama and admired the Antelope's speed, grace, and ability at faking and changing speeds. He could also see that Hutson wasn't only a receiver but was also a complete football player. Lambeau made it his business to sign Hutson and did so before the 1935 season.

Coming into the pros, Hutson suffered a brief crisis of confidence. He just wasn't sure he could make it as a Packer. As a result of the rookie's nervousness, Coach Lambeau held him out of the club's first game that year. But when Green Bay had to go up against the always-tough Chicago Bears in the second game, the coach knew it was time to use his prize rookie.

The Packers had the ball at their own 20-yard line when Don Hutson trotted out on the field for the first time. He was playing left end, but in those days the receivers rarely split out. So he was in tight, alongside the left tackle. The Packers still used the old single wing formation, with the quarterback taking a direct snap from center, much like today's shotgun formation.

With the formation strong to the right, quarterback Arnie Herber took the snap and Hutson broke downfield, using his long, loping stride. Beattie Feathers, the

Bears' speedy halfback, was covering Hutson loosely, but was having no trouble running down the sideline with the rookie. That's when Hutson suddenly showed his talents.

He shot a quick glance over his right shoulder to make it appear as if something was developing there, and as Feathers also turned to look, the rookie shifted into high gear and sped past the astonished defender. Herber let the pass go and Hutson gathered it in past midfield.

Feathers wasn't that far behind when Hutson grabbed the ball, and many fans thought the quick halfback would easily catch the tall receiver. But using his long strides and sprinter's speed, the Alabama Antelope simply outran his pursuer to the end zone.

On his very first play from scrimmage as a pro, Don Hutson had caught an 83-yard touchdown pass, the first of an incredible 100 scoring aerials he would nab during his career. Fittingly, the first one proved to be a game winner, as the Pack took the Bears that afternoon, 7–0.

To this day, many still consider Don Hutson the greatest of them all. He was certainly an innovator. The first of the modern receivers, he was the first to use fakes and changing speeds and the first to run real pass patterns. He went on to create many more great moments, with his circus catches and one-hand grabs. But none could have given Hutson the satisfaction of that first one, a great, game-winning moment the first time he ever touched the football as a pro.

The NFL's senior citizen was old enough to be someone's grandfather in 1970, but even then George Blanda was still a superstar.

Old Man Blanda's Magic Touch

He was a rookie quarterback with the Chicago Bears way back in 1949, but his NFL career never really took off. He was a backup and second stringer for a number of years before the Bears finally cut him. By 1960, he was largely forgotten, but when a new, upstart football league emerged that year, George Blanda was rediscovered.

Already 32 years old, but eager to play regularly after his frustration with the Bears, Blanda won the right to lead the new AFL Houston Oilers. Within a year he was a star quarterback and placekicker, leading the Oilers to the AFL Eastern Division title. In the first ever American Football League championship game, Blanda completed 16 of 31 passes for 301 yards and three touchdowns as the Oilers downed the Los Angeles Chargers, 24–16.

That was the first of three straight AFL title game appearances by the Oilers as George Blanda set a host of league records with his passing. He continued to lead the Oilers for most of the 1960s, but as he neared his fortieth birthday, the team felt it was time for new blood. Old man Blanda was sent to Oakland, but the Raiders already had a fine young quarterback in Daryle Lamonica.

To most observers, Blanda was brought in primarily as a placekicker. Despite his age, he still had one of the best toes in the business. But the veteran also had great confidence in his passing arm, and felt he could still do the job if Lamonica faltered. Plus, that year the Raiders were one of pro football's best, so veteran Blanda was in a good situation.

He even went to the Super Bowl as a Raider, kicking a pair of extra points as Oakland lost to Green Bay in Super Bowl II, 33–14. By 1970, Blanda was openly defying Father Time. He was entering his twenty-second year as a pro and had turned 43 years old. Yet he was still the Raiders' kicker and backup quarterback. Little did he or anyone else know that he was about to amaze the entire football world, producing a succession of great moments that most players only dream about.

The Raiders didn't get off to a good start in 1970, despite predictions that they would win the AFC West. After five games the club had a mediocre 2–2–1 record. Lamonica was again the quarterback, but he was coming under increasing criticism for being a mad bomber, a QB who always wanted to go long and get points in one big strike. So in game six, when Lamonica was injured in the first period, Raider fans cheered as old man Blanda came out on the field.

It didn't take him long to get the arm cranked up. Playing against a good Steeler team, Blanda directed the Raider offense like the seasoned veteran he was. He fired a pair of touchdown passes to Raymond Chester and one to Warren Wells as the Raiders romped, 31–14. It was the first step in Blanda's rise to hero status in Oakland.

A week later, however, Lamonica was back at the helm against the Chiefs. This one was close all the way, but with just three seconds left, the Chiefs had a 17–14 lead. The Raiders had driven to the Kansas City 41, and now George Blanda was sent in to try what would be a 48-yard field goal. It was a long poke for any kicker, especially a 43-year-old one.

But Blanda was used to this kind of pressure. He waited calmly for the snap, then stepped forward and booted the ball. It was up, up, up . . . and good! He had done it, and the three-point field goal gave the Raiders a 17–17 tie. Blanda was on a roll now, and like all the great ones, he wanted the ball. Whether he was throwing or kicking, his confidence was at an all-time high.

A week later he got still another chance to be a hero. This time Lamonica hurt his shoulder in the fourth period with the Raiders trailing the Cleveland Browns, 17–13. After throwing an interception that put Cleveland up, 20–13, it didn't take long for Blanda to

11

go to work. He drove the club downfield and ended the drive with a 14-yard scoring pass to Wells. He then put on his other shoe and kicked the extra point to tie it at 20.

But he wasn't finished yet. When the Raiders got the ball back a final time, he took the club to the Cleveland 45. Now there were just three seconds left, time for one last play. So once again Blanda went from quarterback to placekicker. Only this time the kick would be even longer, some 52 yards. Yet unbelievable as it was, Blanda unloaded a long shot that cleared the crossbar with room to spare. Once again, he had led the Raiders to victory, this time by a 23–20 count.

Now the entire pro football community was singing the praises of the gray-haired old warrior. But how long could his heroics continue? The following week the Raiders were playing the Broncos and trailing, 19–17, with less than four minutes left. This time there was no injury to Lamonica, but the Oakland coaches sent Blanda in anyway. It was getting to be a habit.

Sure enough, the magic continued. With the game once again on the line, the veteran led his club on an 80-yard scoring march. He completed four of six passes on the drive and capped it off with a 20-yard TD toss to end Fred Biletnikoff. The Raiders won it, 24–19.

What could he possibly do for an encore? Fans found out the next week. This time the Raiders were up against the Chargers, and with just seven seconds left, Blanda came on to boot a 16-yard field goal to give his

Blanda's great concentration made him a threat to kick field goals from any place on the field. Here, he gets ready to boot one during his incredible 1970 hot streak.

team a 20–17 victory as well as the lead in the AFC West. It was the fifth straight week that he had come on to tie or win the game in the final seconds.

The Raiders went on to win the division in 1970, and while he continued as a part-time player, George Blanda's contributions were so immense that he was named AFC Player of the Year. No one argued with the choice. After all, most players would give a lot just to produce one game-winning moment during a tough season. Forty-three-year-old George Blanda made it his norm, producing great moments week after week after week after week. It's an achievement still talked about in football circles to this very day.

A Game for All Ages

The 1958 NFL championship game between the New York Giants and Baltimore Colts produced a great moment that continues to have repercussions more than a quarter of a century later. Not only was it a great football game—in fact, many call it the greatest game ever played—but it was also *the* game that really put the National Football League on the map, bringing football the same kind of prominence and attention given baseball and its splashiest show, the World Series.

Why, you ask, did it take a title game played back in 1958 to do all this? After all, the NFL had been putting on championship games since 1933, some of them classics in many ways, and played before large, enthusiastic crowds. That may be true, but to many sports

15

fans, football was still minor league and lacked the mass appeal that baseball, with its rich and glorious tradition, had held for so long.

But when the Giants went up against the Colts on a cold December 28, at Yankee Stadium in New York, everything changed. For openers, the Giants had been one of the NFL's better teams for a number of years. They had won the league title two years earlier, and had also built up a continuing rivalry with the Cleveland Browns, the other Eastern Division powerhouse.

Because of the New York media, the Giants got more than their share of press coverage and attention. Before long, many of the Giants players were almost as well known as those on the great New York Yankee baseball teams. There was graybeard Charley Conerly at quarterback, handsome and talented Frank Gifford at halfback, the powerful Alex Webster at fullback, and veteran Kyle Rote at flanker. It was an explosive offense.

But it was the defense that really gave the Giants their personality. Sculpted by assistant coach Tom Landry, the New York defenders captured the hearts of the fans. Often largely neglected, defensive units usually toiled in anonymity. Not the Giants. They had their fans screaming *"Defense! Defense! Defense!"* every time they came out on the field.

The defense was loaded with highly visible personalities, such as middle linebacker Sam Huff, end Andy Robustelli, tackle Rosey Grier, and safeties Jimmy Patton and Emlen Tunnell among others. These players did not toil in anonymity. They were heroes. So was the entire team after it beat Cleveland twice in the regular season, then whipped the Browns again in the playoff to determine the Eastern Conference champion.

That game was tied at 10–all when Pat Summerall booted a clutch 49-yard field goal in the snow to give the Giants a dramatic victory. That set up the third meeting between New York and Cleveland in a playoff game for the Eastern Conference title. The Giants won, 10–0. Now all that remained between the Giants and another title were the Baltimore Colts. To Giants fans, the Colts were nothing more than brash upstarts. Their team, the Giants, was the team of destiny in 1958.

Indeed, the Colts were something of upstarts. The franchise was begun in 1946 as part of the All-America Football Conference, a rival league that also spawned the Cleveland Browns and San Francisco 49ers. Those two teams as well as the Colts were admitted to the NFL in 1950 after the AAFC folded. But by 1951 the Baltimore franchise was bankrupt and out of business. Two years later, however, Carroll Rosenbloom purchased the defunct Dallas Texans and brought the team to Baltimore. Thus the Colts were reborn. And by 1958 they were good!

The leader of the team was a 25-year-old quarterback named John Unitas. His was the classic success story, the American Dream. Coming out of the University of Louisville in 1955, he was no better than a ninth-round draft choice of the Pittsburgh Steelers. Then, without

17

getting much of a look, he was unceremoniously cut from the team.

When the Colts discovered him, he was playing semipro ball for the Bloomfield Rams and getting the almost embarrassing sum of six dollars a game. But Baltimore saw something they liked, and brought Unitas to camp in 1956 to back up the highly touted George Shaw. Sure enough, an injury to Shaw gave Unitas a chance, and the rest, as they say, is history.

By 1958, Unitas had blossomed into a fine passer and gritty field leader. And to many observers, greatness was just around the corner. In addition, Unitas had the players to back him up. His running backs were L. G. Dupre and Alan "The Horse" Ameche. Lenny Moore, a halfback-flanker, was a potential gamebreaker and dangerous deep receiver.

And then there was Raymond Berry. He was the man Unitas always looked for in clutch situations. Not overly fast or strong, Berry was a master at running patterns and getting open. And if he could get his hands on it, he could catch it. The more Unitas and Berry worked together, the better they became.

The Colts also had their own star defenders, like end Gino Marchetti, tackle Gene "Big Daddy" Lipscomb, linebackers Bill Pellington and Don Shinnick, and defensive back Johnny Sample. When Baltimore won the NFL's Western Conference, knowledgeable football people knew the title game was up for grabs. What they didn't know was just how great a game it would turn out to be.

Emotions ran high from the beginning. For one thing, the Giants had beaten the Colts in the regular season, 24–21. But in that game Unitas was injured and didn't play. In the title game, he made his presence felt on the Colts' first possession when he hit Moore on a long sideline pass that brought the ball to the Giants 25. But the New York defense toughened up, and when Baltimore's Steve Myhra tried a field goal, Sam Huff was right there to block it.

The more than 64,000 fans jamming Yankee Stadium went wild. Their heroes, the defensive unit, had made the first big play of the game. When the offense showed that it could move the ball on the Baltimore "D," the fans were even happier. Though the drive stalled, Pat Summerall came on to boot a 36-yard field goal to give the Giants a 3–0 lead.

But early in the second quarter the Colts got a break. Big Daddy Lipscomb jumped on a Frank Gifford fumble at the New York 20-yard line. Just keeping it on the ground, John Unitas promptly took his team in, and Alan Ameche finally scored from the two. The kick gave Baltimore a 7–3 lead, and the huge crowd was stunned to silence.

Toward the end of the period the Giants threatened, much to the renewed glee of their fans. But just when it looked as if they would regain the lead, Gifford fumbled again, and the Colts recovered inside their own 15.

Quarterback Unitas was still playing it cautiously, keeping the ball mainly on the ground. But the Colt runners were chewing up yardage. They moved into Giant territory, and finally, with the ball at the 15, Johnny U. dropped back and hit Raymond Berry in the end zone for the score. The kick made it a 14–3 ballgame, and there were those beginning to wonder if the extra playoff game with Cleveland had taken too much from the New Yorkers.

It was still 14–3 at the half, but Baltimore coach Weeb Ewbank, wasn't about to start counting chickens.

"I want you to assume we're two touchdowns behind, not eleven points in front," he told his troops. "That's the only way to play it. Get two more touchdowns. Don't just try to protect your lead."

Ewbank knew the Giants were a dangerous team, and in the third period they began to show why. At first the Colts seemed to take up right where they left off. A long drive brought them a first and goal at the three-yard line of the Giants. A score here could put the game on ice.

But the gallant Giant defense proved that it might bend, but it would not break. They made a gutty goal line stand, stopping the Colts four straight times. Asked later why he didn't order a field goal on fourth down, Coach Ewbank said:

"We talked about it, but I wanted to bury them right there with a touchdown."

Taking over on their own five, the Giants showed they weren't about to be buried. After two running plays netted eight yards to the 13, quarterback Charley

Conerly crossed up the Colts. Instead of trying for the first down, he threw deep downfield, where Kyle Rote gathered in the ball and begin heading for the Colts' goal line.

Rote, caught from behind at the 25, suddenly fumbled the ball! But without breaking stride, Giant fullback Alex Webster picked up the loose pigskin and lugged it all the way to the one. Mel Triplett plunged over for the score and Summerall's kick made it a 14–10 game.

As the third period ended and the final session began, the Giants were driving again. Two passes to Bob Schnelker, one of 17 yards and the other of 46, highlighted the march to the Colt 15. The wily Conerly then threw to Frank Gifford for the score that put the Giants on top, with the extra point making it 17–14. The crowd went wild. The momentum had definitely changed and their team had that great defense.

With the crowd exhorting them, the Giant defense began swarming at Unitas, throwing him for losses several times. The clock was winding down and more and more it began to look like another championship for the Giants. With just under three minutes left, the Giants had a third and two play at their own 40. A first down here would undoubtedly allow them to run out the clock.

Conerly gave the ball to Gifford. There was a big pileup of bodies at about the 42. When they unstacked, Gino Marchetti had a fractured ankle, and Big Daddy Lipscomb had Gifford. At first, though, it appeared as if he had the first down. But when he placed the ball, the ref moved it back a couple of inches and it came up short. Now the Giants opted to punt, and although no one knew it then, the game was about to enter a whole new dimension. It was about to go from a fine championship game to a classic, emotional, gut-wrenching football game that no one would ever forget.

Don Chandler's punt was a beauty, high and deep, and the Colts had to fair catch it at their own 14. Now Unitas came out for what could be the last time. There was just 1:56 left, and the Colts were some 86 yards away. But that didn't phase young John Unitas. He was one cool customer as he brought his team onto the field.

Two passes fell incomplete, but Unitas didn't panic. On a third-and-ten play, he calmly went to Lenny Moore for an 11-yard gain and a first down at the Baltimore 25. Now, Unitas and Raymond Berry were about to show the football world why they were destined to be one of the greatest passing combinations of all time.

First the quarterback hit his split end over the middle for a 25-yard gain to midfield. On the next play, Berry made a diving catch of a Unitas aerial at the Baltimore 35. It was another first down, and with time slipping under the one-minute mark, the Colts were getting extremely close to Steve Myhra's field-goal range.

The Giants knew Unitas would throw again and they knew that Berry was a likely target. But the lanky receiver ran such precise, elusive patterns that it was difficult to cover him. Sure enough, Unitas cranked up and found Berry once more, this time all the way down to the Giants' 13-yard line. With just seven seconds left, Myhra came onto the field and booted a 20-yard field goal!

Unbelievably, the Colts had driven 73 yards for the three-pointer that tied the game at 17. But as John Unitas said later, his team was primed for it.

"We were so disgusted with ourselves for the way we'd been playing that when we got on the field for that last series, we struck at the Giants in a kind of blind fury."

Blind fury and great pass patterns by Raymond Berry. Suddenly the game had made history. It was about to go into sudden-death overtime, the first time that had happened in the history of the NFL. What is sudden death? Simple. The first team to score a point in any way (touchdown, field goal, safety) wins the game right then and there. It's the most dramatic situation on a football field.

The Giants got the first break. They won the toss and elected to receive. Baltimore's defense had been inspired by Gino Marchetti, who, despite fracturing his ankle, refused to go to the dressing room for medical attention. He sat on the sidelines exhorting his teammates to stop the New Yorkers.

And stop them they did. A run by Gifford went nowhere. Then a Conerly pass failed. On third down the old quarterback tried to get it himself. He almost made it, but the Colts stopped him less than a yard from the first down. Once again Don Chandler punted, another high, booming kick that backed the Colts all the way to their 20. Unitas came on once more. Only this time he didn't have to worry about the clock.

On first down, halfback L. G. Dupre ran for a first down just over the 30. Then Unitas went long, but the pass for Moore was broken up by Lindon Crow. Another run by Dupre gained a pair, and on a third-down play Unitas hit Ameche for eight and a first down at the 40. The Colts were edging ever so closer.

After a run gained just a couple, Unitas was sacked for an eight-yard loss by Dick Modzelewski. Now the QB faced another third-down call. Dropping back, he looked for his favorite receiver, Raymond Berry. Once again number 82 was open, this time downfield for a 21-yard gain. The Colts were in Giants territory at the 42, and knocking on the door.

Now Unitas showed his brilliant play-calling ability. He crossed up the New York defense by giving the ball to fullback Ameche on a draw, and the Horse rambled for 23 yards before stopping for still another first down at the Giants' 20. The huge crowd was hushed to silence, sensing what seemed more and more inevitable, and praying for some kind of miracle in the form of a turnover.

After a running play failed, Unitas went back to his favorite receiver, and Raymond Berry caught the ball at the nine for another first down. When a run netted just a yard, Unitas fooled the Giants again, passing to Jim Mutscheller, who stepped out of bounds at the one!

It took only one more play. And football fans everywhere have at one time seen the classic picture of Alan Ameche, head down and low to the ground, plunging through a gaping hole in the New York line to score the winning touchdown. The Colts had won it, 23–17, and were World Champs!

The huge crowd at Yankee Stadium might have been stunned by the outcome, but they knew they had seen a great football game. So did the millions watching on national television. They saw professional football at its best, and also saw a young quarterback that many now continue to call the greatest ever.

John Unitas had completed 26 of 40 passes for 349 yards against the toughest defense in the business. And his partner in completions, Raymond Berry, had nailed 12 of them for 178 yards. But it all ended on that one-yard plunge by Ameche. Unitas recalled that one vividly, too.

"When I slapped the ball into Ameche's belly and saw him take off," the quarterback said, "I knew nobody was gonna stop him."

Nobody stopped him, all right, and since that game, nothing has been able to stop the growth of professional football. To many, the 1958 title game between the Giants and the Colts was the one that started it all. Too bad they didn't call it the Super Bowl back then. Because if any game was ever super, that one was.

A Gale Hits Chicago

They call Chicago the Windy City, and anyone who has sat outside to watch the Bears play on a cold Sunday afternoon will undoubtedly agree. But Bear fans don't mind the cold and the wind as long as they're happy with what's happening on the field. And the Monsters of the Midway have given their fans plenty to cheer about down through the years.

Yet of all the great players who have passed through Chicago, from Bronko Nagurski to Walter Payton, none created more magic and pure electricity than Gale Sayers, the mercurial halfback who came out of the University of Kansas to join the Bears in 1965. Despite the fact that his pro career was ultimately cut short by knee injuries, there are still those who call Sayers the greatest running back in the history of the game.

Sayers had it all—speed, elusiveness, and courage.

All it took was a dip or a fake in the open field and he was gone, a threat to score from anywhere on the field every time he touched the football. And no more was this in evidence than in a game with the San Francisco 49ers during Sayers' rookie year. On that day Sayers produced one of the greatest moments in gridiron history.

George Halas, old Papa Bear himself who had founded the franchise back in 1920, was still the coach when Sayers joined the team. Noting how shy and almost withdrawn the rookie runner was, the wily old coach decided not to rush things. In the first two games, he played Sayers only briefly, allowing him to get the feel of the game and to get to know his teammates.

But as soon as the Kansas Comet began to play more, he began to excel and the Bears began to win. In the team's fifth game, a 45–37 victory over the Minnesota Vikings, Sayers made headlines by scoring four times. The National Football League record was six, held jointly by the great Ernie Nevers and Dub Jones, but four was quite an achievement in itself.

By the time the Bears played host to the 49ers in game twelve, Gale Sayers had firmly established himself as not only a top rookie, but also as a great all-around runner. The Bears had won eight straight games after losing the first three while the rookie was getting the feel of things. Now Sayers had scored 16 touchdowns, just four short of the NFL record held by Baltimore's Lenny Moore.

The Bears were playing at Wrigley Field that day, and

27

There are many football fans today who still say no other halfback had the moves of Gale Sayers. In a 1965 game against the Rams, the great Bears runner makes one of his patented "cuts" to elude an L.A. tackler.

a heavy rain had made the field slow and muddy. No one expected a runner like Sayers, who relied on quickness and cutting ability to do well in the mud. But the rookie knew it wouldn't be a problem.

"Most backs cut on the balls of their feet," he said, later. "But I cut on my heels. That helps me keep my footing in the mud."

That claim might have sounded silly to some, but Gale Sayers didn't waste any time proving his point. The first time he touched the ball, he ran 17 yards for a first down. Then, minutes later, when the Bears had the ball again, he took a screen pass from quarterback Rudy Bukich and started upfield.

At first it appeared he would be stopped for a short

gain. But he somehow wriggled through the first wave of defenders and got out in the open field. Then he started using his great moves. Neither the fans, his own teammates, or the startled 49er defenders could believe how well he moved on the muddy field. He faked and danced, sprinted and juked past anyone who tried to stop him. Then he simply outraced the final defenders en route to an 80-yard touchdown romp. And that was only the beginning.

With about five minutes left in the half and the Bears leading, 13–7, Sayers took off again. This time he ran around left end, turned on the speed, and scored once more on a 21-yard jaunt. Minutes later, just before the half ended, the Bears drove downfield again and the rookie halfback made it look easy, scoring from seven yards out, his third TD of the day.

Sayers could have sat down right then and there and still had a great day, but when the third quarter began, he was right back at it. Early in the session he took a Bukich handoff at midfield, faked his way past the first defenders to have a shot at him, then spotted a hole and turned on the afterburner. He sped 50 yards to his fourth score of the day.

Late in the third quarter, the Bears were knocking on the door once again. They had a fourth and goal at the San Francisco one. Normally the power running fullback gets the call here, but quarterback Bukich called on his rookie, and Sayers showed still another dimension of his game. Though just a 200-pounder, he powered into the line like a fullback and drove several bigger men backward as he jackknifed across the goal line for touchdown number five.

Now the Bears had a 40–13 lead, and Coach Halas didn't want to risk an injury to his rookie sensation. He told Sayers he would be restricted to returning punts and kickoffs the remainder of the game. The fans weren't too happy about this, but Sayers wasn't about to let them down. Despite the fog and encroaching darkness, he dropped back to his own 15 to field a San Franciso punt. This time the 49ers were determined to stop him. But how do you stop a magician?

As Sayers weaved his way upfield, almost every 49er had a shot at him. But somehow he escaped them all with dazzling moves in the mud and gloom of Wrigley Field. When he crossed the goal line on an 85-yard return, it was his sixth score of the day, tying the single game record, and his 22nd of the season, giving him a mark all his own.

Sayers's performance brought praise from the entire football community. Friend and foe alike agreed that the swift back from Kansas had already established his greatness in just his rookie year. In addition, his six-touchdown performance against the 49ers would be a moment to remember forever. It was his coach, George Halas, who summed it up best. Halas had seen all the great ones over the years, yet he didn't have to think twice when he said:

"That was the greatest game of football I have ever seen a man play."

It's Up, High Enough,
Deep Enough . . .

Record-setting football players come in all shapes and sizes. But one of the most unusual record-setters ever to make his mark was Tom Dempsey, a placekicking specialist who was with the New Orleans Saints when he made NFL history in 1970. Like so many kickers, Dempsey had his ups and downs, and was with a number of teams before he retired. Yet wherever he went, he had to convince people all over again that he could kick.

Why? Tom Dempsey had a handicap, and for a kicker, a very noticeable one. For openers, he had no fingers on his right hand. But more to the point, he also had no toes on his right foot. And that was his kicking foot!

Dempsey had been born with his handicap, and thus adjusted to it early in life. He was a defensive end in

31

high school and later played both offense and defense at Palomar Junior College. But he made the team because of his kicking abilities. From there it was on to the Atlantic Coast Football League and finally to the NFL with the San Diego Chargers in 1968. By 1970 he was with the Saints.

Using a specially designed shoe to cover his half foot, Dempsey showed good range as a kicker. The front of the shoe was flat and hard, and was often the center of controversy. Whenever Dempsey kicked an important field goal, it seemed that the rival coach tried to have the shoe banned. But both the shoe and Dempsey stayed on.

On November 8, 1970, the Saints were in a nip-and-tuck battle with the Detroit Lions. With just 13 seconds left, Detroit's Errol Mann booted an 18-yard field goal to give his team a 17–16 lead. By the time the Saints ran the kickoff back and completed one pass to their own 45, there were just two seconds left.

Most fans figured there was time for a desperation pass, nothing more. But the Saints coaching staff fooled everyone. They sent Tom Dempsey out to try a 63-yard field goal. If he made it, the kick would be an NFL record. But as Dempsey himself once said.

"I don't go out to try field goals. I go out to make them."

But a 63-yarder? Some of the Lions couldn't even believe it, and at the snap they hardly rushed Dempsey. One who did was all-pro Alex Karras, and he just missed blocking the kick. But Dempsey hit it and hit it good. The ball soared high and deep, and most importantly, straight. The referee raised both arms. The kick was good! Dempsey had set a new NFL record and won a game for his team in the process. You couldn't ask for any better than that.

"I knew I could kick it sixty-three yards," Dempsey said later. "I just wasn't sure I could kick it straight. I tried to shut the pressure out of my mind and concentrate on getting the ball up so it wouldn't be blocked."

Tom Dempsey did it, all right. A most unusual kicker, he showed everyone that he really had no handicap at all!

Welcome to a New Era— A Super One

For diehard football fans it still seems as if it happened yesterday. But by 1986, there had already been twenty of these games, twenty games since professional football entered still another new era. The subject is perhaps the biggest single sports extravaganza of them all: the Super Bowl. And as millions of people watched the Chicago Bears steamroll the New England Patriots in Super Bowl XX, many fans were thinking back to that first super game some two decades earlier. No matter what the outcome of the game that day between the Green Bay Packers and the Kansas City Chiefs, it will always remain one of the great moments in gridiron history.

In reality, the genesis of the Super Bowl occurred back in 1960, when a second professional football league was formed to rival the established National

Football League. At first, most people thought the American Football League (AFL) was doomed to failure. After all, real football fans just wouldn't buy an inferior product, and the NFL had had a difficult enough time establishing itself as a prime television attraction.

But the AFL was formed by a group of young, energetic businessmen who not only worked hard to make the league survive, but had the financial backing to withstand the early losses. While most of the players the first year or two were NFL retreads, minor leaguers, and veterans coming back for a last hurrah, it wasn't long before the AFL began acquiring quality. They started bidding for the top players leaving the college ranks and before long were putting an attractive, quality product on the football field.

There are those who feel the AFL really came of age with the signing of quarterback Joe Namath by the New York Jets in 1965. Namath not only received perhaps the largest contract ever given a pro football player up to that time (his deal was reported to be in the $400,000 range), but he gave the AFL a dynamic, charismatic player who could put people in the seats. But he wasn't the only one. By the mid 1960s it was obvious that the AFL was here to stay, and both leagues wanted to do something to stabilize the escalating salaries and bidding war for players.

Thus the merger was drawn. It wouldn't take effect fully until 1970, when the two leagues would become one big National Football League. But the pre-merger agreement included the playing of a championship game between the best of the NFL and AFL. The first was scheduled after the 1966 season.

At first it was to be called simply the AFL-NFL Championship Game. But one day Lamar Hunt, the owner of the Kansas City Chiefs and perhaps the moving force behind the entire AFL, saw his little girl bouncing a rubber ball off a wall. As she was bouncing it, she told her daddy that it was a super ball.

From that innocent remark, Hunt created the name of the Super Bowl, and that has become a name everyone in the country recognizes immediately. And Hunt had plenty of reason to be involved in that first big game. His Kansas City Chiefs had won the AFL championship, defeating the Buffalo Bills, 31–7. The Chiefs would be meeting the powerful Green Bay Packers, the closest thing to a football dynasty in the 1960s. The Pack had defeated the Dallas Cowboys, 34–27, to get into that first Super Bowl.

Green Bay was coached by Vince Lombardi, already a living legend, and a man who had come to Green Bay in the late 1950s, when the Packers were a bunch of ragtag losers.

"See this," he said, the first day he was Packers coach. "This is a football. And before we're through we're gonna run it down everybody's throat."

Lombardi was true to his word. By 1960 he had the Packers in the championship game. And while they lost a close one to the Philadelphia Eagles, the team was for real. They proved it the following year, winning the

NFL title with a 37–0 drubbing of the New York Giants. They also won the league crown in 1962, 1965, and 1966. To most fans, Lombardi's Packers were the best team in the world. When they whipped the Cowboys for the NFL title, that was *the* championship. The Super Bowl game against the Chiefs figured to be little more than an exhibition.

The Packers were loaded with future Hall of Famers. There was quarterback Bart Starr, running back Jim Taylor, receivers Boyd Dowler and Carroll Dale, plus a super offensive line led by guards Jerry Kramer and Fuzzy Thurston.

As for the defense, they just might have been the heart of the team. All-Stars at nearly every position, it included rock-ribbed performers such as end Willie Davis; tackle Henry Jordan; linebackers Ray Nitschke, Dave Robinson, and Lee Roy Caffey; and defensive backs Willie Wood, Herb Adderley, and Bob Jeter. It was hard for most NFL fans to visualize the Chiefs doing anything with the Packer defense.

But Kansas City had some fine individual performers also. Their quarterback was Len Dawson, who had sat the bench for several years in the NFL but blossomed into a fine passer at K.C. Mike Garrett, a Heisman Trophy-winning halfback out of University of Southern California was the team's top runner. Otis Taylor was a gamebreaker at wide receiver, and the offensive line was big and tough.

The defense also had some tough customers, such as end Jerry Mays, tackle Buck Buchanan, linebackers

Bobby Bell and E. J. Holub, and safeties Bobby Hunt and Johnny Robinson. Still, as game time approached, the Packers were heavy favorites. No one gave the Chiefs much of a chance.

There were some 61,946 fans in the 100,000-seat Los Angeles Coliseum to witness this history-making event for professional football. When the Packers received the ball, many fans thought they would drive right down the field for a score. But after getting a first down, the Chiefs stormed through to sack Bart Starr twice, forcing the Packers to punt.

K.C. couldn't move either, and they punted back to Green Bay, giving the Packers the ball at their own 20. Now Bart Starr went to work. He began throwing the ball, completing passes to tight end Marv Fleming and running back Elijah Pitts. Finally the Packers moved to the Kansas City 37, where they had a third and three. Starr dropped back to pass again.

He had already lost his best wide receiver, Boyd Dowler, to a shoulder injury, and now looked to substitute Max McGee. McGee was a veteran, coming to the end of a fine career, and he really hadn't expected to play. So the night before the game he had stayed out very late. Now he was in the game full-time and cutting across the middle looking for the ball.

Starr fired. McGee was running at the 19 and the ball was a little behind him. He reached back and grabbed it and ran into the end zone. Don Chandler's extra-point try was good, and with 8:56 gone in the first quarter, Green Bay had a 7–0 lead. But by the end of the period it was still 7–0, and many Packer fans wondered why their team wasn't running up the score against these AFL upstarts.

Shortly after the second period began, NFL fans had more reason to worry. Kansas City began driving from their own 34, quarterback Dawson using "play-action" passes—that is, faking to his backs before throwing—and it seemed to confuse the Packer defense. The mixture of runs and play-action passes brought the ball to the Packer 38.

Then Dawson fired a beautiful pass (down the left sideline), to Otis Taylor and the big receiver took it all the way to the Green Bay seven. From there, Dawson flipped a quickie to fullback Curtis McClinton, who rambled in for the score. The kick made it a 7–7 game, and almost everyone watching was stunned by the sudden turn of events.

Green Bay tried to strike back quickly, and for a second it looked as if they would. Starr faked to his fullback, then lofted what appeared to be a 64-yard TD pass to Carroll Dale. But there was a flag. The Pack was penalized for illegal procedure, and the pass brought back.

With a third and six on their own 31, it looked like Green Bay was in trouble. But Starr calmly completed a pass to McGee at the 42 for a first down. From there the Pack began driving again. Mixing his passes with runs, Starr brought his club to the K.C. 14. That's when he called the famous Packer sweep. Jim Taylor took the ball and followed his great guards, Kramer

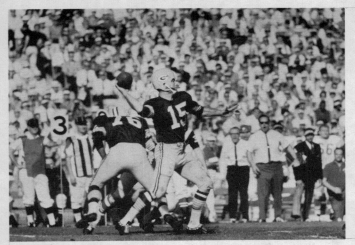

Whenever a big play was needed by the Green Bay offense in Super Bowl I, quarterback Bart Starr was ready to deliver.

and Thurston, all the way to the end zone for a score. The kick made it a 14–7 game.

Still, the Chiefs wouldn't quit. They drove again late in the period, and with less than a minute left in the half, Mike Mercer kicked a 31-yard field goal to make it a 14–10 game at the half. The Chiefs were surprisingly in it, and had to be thinking upset as they left the field.

At halftime the Packers realized they were not in a cakewalk. They were in a football game. And some observers were beginning to lean toward the Chiefs. The late Buddy Young, a former NFL running back, was heard to quip, "Age and the heat will get the Packers in the second half."

As for Lombardi, the great coach read the riot act to his defense. Wary of Dawson's play-acting passing (something that wasn't used much in the NFL at the time), the defense was being tentative.

"Stop grabbing and start tackling," Lombardi told his troops, and all of the defenders began exhorting each other to go out and start knocking people down.

Though the Packers were fired up, the Chiefs began moving the ball again. They got to their own 49 and had a third and five. That's when the Packers decided to

Veteran receiver Max McGee, not expected to play, turned out to be the unlikely hero of Super Bowl I. Here, McGee takes a Bart Starr aerial toward the end zone in the Packers 335–10 victory over the Kansas City Chiefs.

blitz, and Dawson was forced to hurry his pass. It was picked off by Willie Wood, and he had open field in front of him, returning it 50 yards all the way to the five-yard line. A play later Elijah Pitts powered into the end zone, and Chandler's kick made it 21–10. It was a big turnover. It renewed the Packer confidence and took some of the air out of the Chiefs' balloon. In effect, it turned the game around.

By the end of the third period the Packers had scored again on a 13-yard Starr-to-McGee pass. The kick made it 28–10, pretty much putting the game out of reach. The icing on the cake came in the final session, as Green Bay drove 80 yards for the last score and a 35–10 victory in the first Super Bowl ever.

Bart Starr was the game's Most Valuable Player on the strength of 16 completions in 23 attempts for 250 yards and two scores. Losing coach Hank Stram agreed with the choice.

"It was Starr's uncanny ability to come up with the successful third-down play that was the single difference between the two teams."

Indeed, Starr was successful on 10 of 13 third-down conversions. Losing quarterback Len Dawson saw Willie Wood's interception as the turning point, that and Packer football.

"That interception gave them the momentum," Dawson said. "Then they took the football and shoved it down our throats."

That's what Vince Lombardi was all about. And it was a magical moment as the veteran coach received

42

the winning trophy from NFL Commissioner Pete Rozelle. Fittingly, the Packers were to also win Super Bowl II, the following year. It was Lombardi's final game as Packers coach and the last hurrah for an aging team that will be remembered as one of the greatest ever. Today, the winning team in the Super Bowl receives the Vince Lombardi Trophy in memory of the late coach who did so much for the pro game.

It was never more in evidence than in that first Super Bowl. Lombardi's winning smile beamed to millions of viewers across the land and his Packers produced a truly great moment in football.

Those Moments
in the Trenches

Perhaps the most unheralded performers on a football field are the linemen, those huge, strong, tough men who collide viciously at every snap of the ball. It may seem difficult to believe, but these men are fully capable of turning a great moment. It may not happen with them as often as it does with a back, or a receiver, and sometimes it can only be appreciated by peers. But it does happen. Here are a couple of examples.

In the late 1960s and early 1970s, the Minnesota Vikings had a powerful football team, a team spearheaded by a tough defensive unit. The front four of that unit were nicknamed the Purple People Eaters. Perhaps the most dangerous player in that unit was tackle Alan Page, a 6-foot-4, 245-pound terror who had been an all-American at Notre Dame. By 1971, Page was in his fifth season and in the prime of his football life.

The Vikes were playing an important late-season game with Detroit and leading, 14–3, midway through the second period. But the Lions were moving the football and showing signs of swinging the momentum their way. That is, until Alan Page got mad.

Page was known as one of the quickest tackles in the league, so quick that one quarterback put it this way: "He gets into the opposing backfield before the ball does."

About this time, Page made one of his patented moves and burst into the Lion backfield. The problem was that the ref didn't like what Page did and penalized him and the Vikes 15 yards for a personal foul. Then on the next play, when Page hit Lions quarterback Greg Landry just after he threw the ball, the yellow flag dropped again. This time Page was called for roughing the passer, advancing the ball another 15 yards toward the Minnesota goal line. Two straight penalties and Alan Page was furious.

He couldn't take it out on the ref, so he turned his attention to the Lions. At the snap he brushed aside a big offensive lineman as if he were a rag doll and ran straight at Landry, sacking him for a loss of nine yards. On the next play the Lions double-teamed Page, but he kept driving until one of them held him in desperation. The ensuing penalty pushed the Lions back another 15 yards.

It was still second down and Landry dropped back again. Once more number 88 led the charge, forcing the quarterback to hurry his throw and miss his target. The

Big, fast, and strong, Alan Page was capable of dominating a game from his defensive tackle position. An integral part of the Purple People Eaters front four, Page helped make the Vikings one of the top NFL teams of the 1970s.

Lions got a break when a Viking penalty kept the down the same. Landry looked to pass again, but before he could even pick out his receiver, Alan Page came thundering in and sacked him for another loss of nine yards.

On third and long, Landry thought he could catch the Vikings by surprise. He called a draw play, dropping back as if to pass, then giving the ball to halfback Altie Taylor. But Taylor was caught dead in his tracks, caught by 245 pounds of determination—Alan Page.

On one series of downs, Alan Page had pushed the Lions back 33 yards. All by himself. He helped set the stage for a 29–10 Viking victory, and in the process had created a great moment that was appreciated by all who witnessed it.

"Alan was just showing some of his potential," said Viking coach Bud Grant. "It shows just what he's capable of doing. Sometimes his power is frightening."

Another powerful player of the same era was Willie Lanier, the bruising middle linebacker of the Kansas City Chiefs. Though linebackers are not really in the trenches, Lanier played the kind of game that often put him at the point of the action. His Hall of Fame credentials attest to that fact.

But on a cold December day in 1969, when the Chiefs were at windy Shea Stadium in New York meeting the New York Jets, Willie Lanier's determination and emotion helped create a great moment that his teammates will never forget.

It was a playoff game, the winner advancing to the

AFL title game, so the stakes were high. K.C. had a slim lead, but quarterback Joe Namath had his Jets driving. A score would give the New Yorkers the lead, and they would be tough to catch on their home turf. When the Jets got a first and goal inside the 10, it looked as if they would get the go-ahead score. K.C. cornerback Emmit Thomas recalled what happened next.

"Willie had already called the defensive signals and we had broken our huddle. It was pretty quiet out there. I guess most of us were lost in our thoughts. Suddenly Willie just seemed to snap. He was almost hysterical, crying and screaming. He began running back and forth, urging us, ordering us, begging us to stop them. I remember there were tears running down his cheeks. He reminded us how hard we had worked since last July for this moment, and he said we couldn't throw it away."

When the Jets broke their huddle and came to the line, Willie Lanier looked at them and the torrent of emotion poured forth again.

"THEY'RE NOT GOING TO SCORE!" he screamed. "THEY'RE NOT GOING TO SCORE!"

"Willie had gotten to all of us," Emmitt Thomas said. "Suddenly I yelled it, then Jerry Mays yelled it, then Buck Buchanan, then Bobby Bell. All of us. We just kept saying it, over and over."

On first down, Namath gave the ball to fullback Matt Snell, who looked to power his way up the middle. But he was met by a group of Chiefs tacklers, led by Lan-

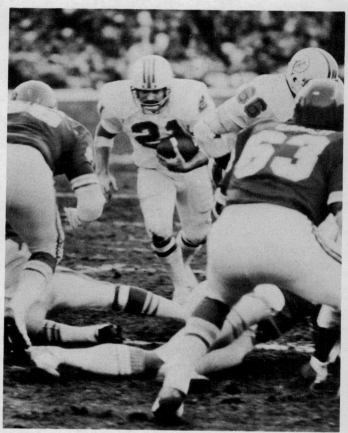

Kansas City middle linebacker Willie Lanier was like the Rock of Gibraltar throughout his career. In this game against Miami, Lanier (63) gets ready to close the gap and stop Dolphins ballcarrier, Jim Kiick.

ier, who drove him back for no gain. On second down, Namath gave the ball to halfback Bill Mathis. The blocking was there, but the determined Chiefs broke the wedge as Buchanan, Bell, and Lanier plowed Mathis under for nothing again. Now it was third down.

Namath was no fool. He saw that the middle of the K.C. line was playing with incredible determination and almost superhuman strength. He decided to try a rollout. But the defense reacted, and as the gimpy-kneed Namath looked for a receiver, he was buried for a big loss.

On fourth down, the Jets had to settle for a field goal. It was a moral victory for the Chiefs, and they went on to score a 13–6 win, which was a stepping stone to an eventual Super Bowl triumph that year. But none of that might have happened if Willie Lanier hadn't produced his own kind of great moment. As one of the Chiefs' defenders recalled:

"Willie did it. He got our juices flowing. If he didn't fire us up on that goal line, we might have quit right there. I remember thinking that if they scored, we were done. But Willie took over. He wouldn't let them score. And he gave the feeling to all of us."

Great moments. Some are flashy, out front, right there for the whole country to see. Others are more subtle, perhaps not even noticeable to many fans. But those moments can be just as important. They can turn a game, even a whole season, around. Alan Page and Willie Lanier were both impact players, fully capable of creating a great moment in football.

The Immaculate Reception

In 1972, Franco Harris was a rookie fullback with the Pittsburgh Steelers. It was to be a memorable year for the big, fast runner out of Penn State. He was with a team that was quickly approaching greatness, a team that would play in and win four Super Bowls in the years 1976–80. And Franco, too, was on the verge of that same greatness.

After a slow start, he came on to gain more than 1,000 yards that year, including a streak of six 100-yard games in a row. He was a power runner who also had the ability to go outside and outrun many of the defensive backs in the league.

Even though they were a young, developing team, the Steelers finished the 1972 season with an 11–3 mark, good enough for the AFC Central Division Championship and a trip to the playoffs. Even more unbelievable was the fact that it was the club's first title in the 40-year history of the franchise.

Franco had finished the season with 1,055 yards on 188 carries, for an impressive 5.6 yards per carry average, the best in the league. He also caught 21 passes for 180 yards and scored 11 touchdowns, 10 of them on the ground. When it was over, he was named AFC Rookie of the Year and was part of an explosive offense that accounted for 343 points.

But the Steelers wouldn't have it easy in their first playoff game. They would be meeting the always powerful Oakland Raiders. Both clubs were known for their strong defenses. The Raiders were always a team that beat up on the opposition, and the Steel Curtain defense of Pittsburgh was just becoming a force in the NFL.

As expected, the game was a defensive battle from the first, neither team able to move the ball with any consistency. Oakland's quarterback Daryle Lamonica, was playing with a bad case of flu, and Pittsburgh's third-year QB, strong-armed Terry Bradshaw, wasn't having much luck, either. As for Franco Harris, the tough Oakland line was keying on him and preventing him from breaking any long ones.

By the fourth quarter, Pittsburgh held a 6–0 lead, scoring only on a pair of field goals. But the Steel Curtain continued to throw a blanket over the Raider offense. Maybe the six points would be enough?

Late in the fourth period it was still 6–0, and the

Raiders began hoping for a miracle. Midway through the period they had replaced the flu-ridden Lamonica with young Ken Stabler, a scrambler and a gambler. Could the man who would become known as the Snake be able to put some points on the board?

There were just minutes remaining when Stabler began moving his ballclub. A pass to Mike Siani brought the ball to the Pittsburgh 30. As Stabler dropped back again, the Steelers blitzed, hoping to nail him before he could get another pass off. But the Snake saw it coming and rolled to his left. Suddenly he had an open shot down the sideline and he took it. The Steelers didn't recover in time, and Stabler ran it in for a touchdown! George Blanda's extra point made it a 7–6 game. With 1:13 left, the Steelers were in deep trouble. They had come so far, only to fall behind in the final minute. Right then, in the minds of most observers, the Steelers had two chances—slim and none.

Their only real chance was to get into field-goal range, and they would have to do that quickly. What no one knew then, no one could possibly have known, was that one of the greatest moments in football history was about to happen, a once-in-a-lifetime event. And the central figure in it would be the rookie fullback, Franco Harris.

The Steelers got the football deep in their own territory. Quarterback Bradshaw, running the hurry-up offense, completed a pair of passes to bring his team to their own 40. But then the drive stalled. Bradshaw missed three straight passes and was faced with a fourth-and-ten with just 22 seconds left. The next play could be the Steelers' last of the season.

After conferring with Coach Chuck Noll, Bradshaw returned and took the snap. He dropped back and looked downfield, hoping to complete a pass and still have enough time left for a field-goal try. When he couldn't find primary receiver Barry Pearson, Bradshaw scrambled to his right for more time. Then he spotted halfback John Fuqua open at the Oakland 37. He cranked and fired.

But just as Fuqua reached for the ball, Raider safety Jack Tatum hit him with one of his patented hard shots. Fuqua went one way and the ball another. The huge crowd at Three Rivers Stadium let out a collective groan. The game, it appeared, was over. Some of the Raider defenders were already jumping up and down in celebration.

But wait a minute! If the game was over, why was Franco Harris running full speed toward the Raider goal line? Quickly more and more eyes focused on big number 32. Sure enough, he had the football. Only a few had actually seen what had happened. The ball had bounced away from Fuqua and Tatum, when Franco, trailing the play, grabbed it in flight just before it hit the ground.

Even the Raiders were slow to react as the big guy rambled toward the goal line. Only safety Jimmy Warren had a shot at him around the 10, but Franco brushed right past him into the end zone. Then the

An alert Franco Harris heads downfield, following the play that was to become known as the "Immaculate Reception." Harris took a deflected pass in for the winning touchdown in the Steelers playoff victory over the Oakland Raiders.

officials had to study the play for several minutes, making sure both Fuqua and Tatum had touched the ball. If only Fuqua had touched it, Franco's catch would have been illegal. But once it was determined that both had touched it, then it was . . . a touchdown! The Steelers had scored. The Steelers had won. The Immaculate Reception, as it would come to be called, had stunned everyone.

"I wasn't even supposed to be there," Franco said later. "I was running to block for Fuqua, I saw the collision, then saw the ball coming at me. I caught it just below the knees, never broke stride, and just ran as fast as I could."

It was a miracle finish of the first rank, and it quickly became a permanent part of Steeler folklore. Pittsburgh didn't win the Super Bowl that year. They lost the AFC title game to unbeaten Miami. But it was a prelude of things to come. The Steelers would go on to win four of the big ones, and Franco Harris would become the National Football League's third best all-time ground gainer at the time of his retirement.

But no one knew all this in 1972. All they knew then was that they had just witnessed one of the greatest moments in gridiron history, a play that happens once in a lifetime, an Immaculate Reception that will never be duplicated.

And an Old Fullback
Will Lead Them

Not many running backs are still active after the age of 30. And those over 30 generally are on the downslide, playing out the string, maybe just seeing spot duty for a final season or two. There are some exceptions, of course, but not too many.

Now take a running back over 30, a player always considered a maverick, a nonconformist, and sometimes a troublemaker, and have him sit out an entire season in a contract dispute. Would you really want this player back? And if so, would he really be able to make a valuable contribution to a team?

The answer on both counts is yes. Yes, because it really happened, and because the player not only became a star once again, but produced a great moment that only a great player was capable of producing. Football fans by now will probably have guessed it.

The player was John Riggins, the bruising fullback of the Washington Redskins.

Riggins had always been a maverick, ever since beginning his career with the New York Jets in the early 1970s. He came out of the University of Kansas, where he broke many of Gale Sayers's rushing records, and he was an immediate success as a hard-running fullback with the speed to go outside and the agility to fake linebackers and defensive backs.

Yet he always did things his own way. One year he came to camp with a radical Mohawk haircut. He often antagonized the coaches with his antics at practice, and he rubbed the front office the wrong way because he was a tough and insistent negotiator at contract time. So the Jets finally shipped him to Washington.

But he wasn't strictly a badboy. On the field, he generally produced, often in all-pro style. He became the Jets' first 1,000-yard rusher and repeated that milestone with the 'Skins. Then, in 1980, with the final year of his five-year pack looming ahead, Riggins wanted to renegotiate. When the team refused, the big fullback went home and stayed home for the entire season.

By the summer of 1981, the Redskins had a new coach in Joe Gibbs, and one of his first questions was whether John Riggins wanted to rejoin the team. And if so, could he regain his old form at the advanced age of 31? With timing and conditioning so important for a runner, a player over 30 who hadn't played in over a year might not be able to make it back.

But surprisingly, Riggins said he wanted to give it another try. He was tired of staying home and painting his house. So he signed a contract and went back to work. He wasn't quite the Riggins of old, but he seemed to get better as the season wore on and he finished with a respectable 714 yards rushing.

Then came 1982, and the Redskins had a contending team. There was a mammoth offensive line averaging 270 pounds; a slick, mobile quarterback in veteran Joe Theismann; and several quick, sure-handed pass receivers. With all this firepower, Coach Gibbs also went to a one-back running attack. The one back: John Riggins.

With a balanced offense, Riggins didn't have to overwork himself. Coach Gibbs preferred the passing game, but the big guy came through whenever asked. The problem was that the season was split by a players' strike and shortened to just nine games. The Redskins proved themselves in those nine games, finishing with an 8–1 record, and were one of the favorites in a special Super Bowl tournament devised to compensate for the strike-shortened season.

As for John Riggins, in those nine games he gained 553 yards, a respectable amount. Had the season gone the full 16, he would have been right around 1,000. But with the Super Bowl tournament coming up, Riggins saw his role as something more. Never too shy to speak up, he approached his coach and made a brash statement: "Give me the ball 20 or 25 times a game and we'll win it," he announced.

Maybe Coach Gibbs saw something in Riggins' eyes, or maybe he felt it was time to alter the team's game plan to throw opposing defenses off. Gibbs decided to go with his running attack, especially if his team got an early lead.

And that's exactly what happened in playoff games against Detroit, Minnesota, and Dallas. Each time, it wound up with John Riggins controlling the tempo of the action, especially in the second half when the Skins had the lead. He was almost unstoppable, a pile driver who kept hammering at the enemy lines without tiring. The 'Skins won all three games to take the NFC title, and John Riggins had gained 444 yards on 98 carries. So he was averaging 148 yards on nearly 33 carries a game. That's a workload that most 22-year-olds would find difficult, let alone a 32-year-old fullback.

But Riggins thrived on it, and as the Redskins prepared to meet the Miami Dolphins in Super Bowl XVII, the question was could the old man do it again. "I thought he could do it all year long," said 295-pound Redskin tackle Joe Jacoby. "He just needed to get the ball a little more."

Coach Gibbs was also elated at Riggins' dominance. He admitted that everyone, including the fullback, had wondered about his comeback the year before, especially when he didn't play well in the first part of the season. "All of us, including John, wondered if he was through," Gibbs said. "Obviously, he wasn't."

Now it was Super Bowl time, and if a player is ever going to produce a great moment, there isn't a better

An imposing sight for any defender: fullback John Riggins of the Redskins under a head of steam. Agile as well as powerful, the veteran runner gained 166 yards against Miami in Super Bowl XVII.

stage upon which to do it. There would be more than 103,000 spectators jamming the Rose Bowl in Pasadena, California, to see the 'Skins and the Dolphins. And if John Riggins was feeling any pressure, he certainly wasn't showing it. In fact, he was proving all over again that he was the same old, unpredictable flake.

First, he broke a two-year moratorium on speaking with the press. In his first mass interview, he was amusing and humorous, as well as honest. Then, two days before the game, the 'Skins had a big party with casual dress the order of the day. John Riggins showed up in a top hat, white tie, and tails, as well as carrying a formal walking stick. He helped loosen everyone up.

But once the game started, he was all business. The Dolphins were lead by their "Killer Bees" defense, named because more than half the starting defenders had last names beginning with the letter B. They would be geared to stop John Riggins.

It was the Miami offense, however, that surprised everyone early in the game. On just their second possession, the Dolphins struck when quarterback David Woodley hit wide receiver Jimmy Cefalo for a 76-yard scoring play. The kick made it 7–0, and it stayed that way through the remainder of the first quarter.

The second period turned out to be a stalemate. First there was an exchange of field goals, making it a 10–3 game. With six minutes left, the Redskins drove into Miami territory. Riggins caught a fifteen-yard swing pass along the way, and the 'Skins finally scored on a four-yard pass from Theismann to Alvin Garrett. Mark Moseley's extra point tied the game at ten.

But before the Redskins could savor their score, they were shocked to silence by a 98-yard kickoff return by Miami's Fulton Walker, giving the Dolphins the lead once again. The half ended with the Dolphins in front, 17–10.

Riggins had carried the ball 17 times in the first half and did a good job, though he really didn't have an impact on the game. Would Washington still go to him in the second half, though they were trailing, or would the game plan take them back to the air?

The momentum of the game began swinging in the third period. The only scoring was a 20-yard field goal by Moseley which brought the score to 17–13, but the Redskin defense had begun to stop the Dolphins cold, while John Riggins and his offensive line were beginning to ramble through the heart of the Dolphin defense.

Early in the fourth period, the Redskins were still trailing. They got the ball at their own 48. Riggins carried twice for eight yards, then Clarence Harmon ran for one. So it was a fourth-and-one on the Miami 43. The 'Skins decided to go for it. And as all 103,000 fans at the Rose Bowl, the millions watching on television, and the players on both teams all knew, the ball went to John Riggins. Only he didn't plunge straight up the middle for the first down.

Instead, Riggins ran left behind a block by Jacoby, cut to the outside where he brushed past cornerback

Don McNeal, who had been suckered out of position by a fake, then raced the remaining distance to the goal line. In doing so, he showed everyone that the old man still had his great speed. The score and kick put the Redskins where they wanted to be, up by a 20–17 count.

Now the 'Skins began controlling the clock, and that meant running John Riggins right up the gut. At one point Big John carried five straight times and kept pushing the Dolphins backward. The final Redskin drive consumed some six minutes, with Riggins doing the bulk of the heavy work. When quarterback Theismann hit Charley Brown with a short six-yard TD pass, there were less than two minutes remaining. Moseley's kick made it 27–17, and that's the way it ended.

There was little doubt who would get the Most Valuable Player trophy. Old man John Riggins had carried the ball 38 times and had gained 166 yards, both Super Bowl records. That made his total in four postseason games, 610 yards on 136 carries, more yards than he had gained in nine regular season games. Topping it with his great performance in the Super Bowl was surely a magical moment.

After the game, the winning team got the traditional phone call from President Ronald Reagan. John Riggins was one of the 'Skins who spoke with the President. Afterward, facing the press, he was true to character when he said: "Ronald Reagan may be President, but today I'm king."

The Man You Never Count Out

His reputation began back in 1975, when he was just a second-string sophomore quarterback at Notre Dame. Up to that time, there was still a big question about his ultimate ability, whether he would become a solid starting quarterback for the Fighting Irish. After all, when he first joined the varsity that year, he was listed as the number seven quarterback on the team's preseason depth chart.

But he worked his way up to number two and saw some early season action behind Rick Slager. He came off the bench in a game against a weak Northwestern team and led the Irish to a 31–7 victory. But it was in game five against North Carolina that the legend of Joe Montana got its start.

Slager was at the helm for most of the game, but with just six minutes left and the Irish trailing, 14–6, Coach

Dan Devine made the move to Montana. All that Montana did in those final six minutes was hit on three of four passes for a big 129 yards and one touchdown, and set up another, as the Irish won it, 21–14.

A week later it happened again. This time Notre Dame was trailing the Air Force, 30–10, when Joe got the call. Playing with coolness and confidence, Joe marched the Irish downfield three times, completing seven passes for 134 yards and two scores. The Irish won, 31–30, and Joe Montana was suddenly the miracle worker, a Comeback Kid who could do no wrong.

After missing the 1976 season to a shoulder injury, Joe was up to his old tricks again in '77. Replacing Rusty Lisch in the third quarter with the Irish trailing Purdue, 24–14, Joe Montana completing nine of 14 passes in just sixteen minutes of action. That was good for 154 yards and 17 fourth-quarter points as the Irish won it, 31–24.

Joe not only engineered come-from-behind victories that year, he also led the Irish to a 38–10 victory over previously unbeaten Texas in the Cotton Bowl, a game that gave the once-beaten Irish the National Championship. There were some ups and downs in Joe's senior year of 1978, but he never lost his reputation as the Comeback Kid.

He did it against Pittsburgh that year. With the Irish trailing 17–7 in the final session, Montana completed seven straight passes which led to 19 points and a 26–17 victory. And in the Cotton Bowl game that year, the

It was at Notre Dame that Joe Montana first got his reputation as the Comeback Kid. Here he is in action during one of his comeback miracles against Houston in the Cotton Bowl game of 1978.

Irish trailed Houston 34–12, late in the third period. Once again Joe Montana went to work.

Three times in the waning minutes he marched the Irish downfield for scores, the final coming with no time left on the clock, to give the Irish a 35–34 win. He had completed 13 passes during the surge, threw for a score, ran for another, and fired a pair of two-point conversions. It was his greatest finish of all and a great way to end his college career.

Montana certainly had all the earmarks of a great pro. Yet there were some who felt he didn't have all the credentials, in spite of the many miracles he had worked. They said he was inconsistent, and that his arm wasn't strong enough. When he was finally picked in the college draft, it was in the third round, and the team that picked him was the San Francisco 49ers, a club that had a 2–14 record in 1978.

But the 49ers had a new coach in Bill Walsh, and he knew just the kind of club and the kind of offense he wanted. He wouldn't rush it, just as he wouldn't rush Joe Montana. Joe played sparingly in 1979, throwing just 23 passes all year. The next season, he split duties with Steve DeBerg, as the club improved to 6–10. Joe completed a 64.5 percent of his passes and threw for 15 TDs against just nine intercepts.

There were a lot of good young players with the team in 1981, and to settle any controversy before it started, the club traded Steve DeBerg to Denver. Joe Montana was now the number one quarterback.

"We felt Joe was our quarterback of the future all

along," Coach Walsh said. "We worked him in slowly to give him steady exposure to the league, but not to rush him."

With Joe throwing to a pair of great receivers, Dwight Clark and Freddie Solomon; a good running attack; and a revamped, aggressive defense, the 49ers were the surprise of the football world in 1981. They won the NFC West with a 13–3 record as Joe Montana had a brilliant year. He completed 311 of 488 passes for 3,565 yards and 19 touchdowns. He had arrived.

In his first ever playoff, Joe was brilliant. as the 'Niners defeated the New York Giants, 38–24. Joe hit on 20 of 31 for 304 yards and two scores. Now came the big one, the Dallas Cowboys for the NFC title and the right to go to the Super Bowl.

It was a hard-fought contest from the beginning, and the lead changed hands several times. Finally, midway through the fourth quarter, the Cowboys jumped in front again, 27–21. There were less than five minutes left when the 'Niners got the ball again but way back on their own 11-yard line. To win the game, Joe Montana would have to be the Comeback Kid once more.

After two plays, Joe had a third and four. He calmly tossed a six-yard pass to Solomon for a first down. From there, he moved the club downfield against the tough Dallas defense, mixing running plays with 10- and 12-yard passes to Clark and Solomon. Finally he had a first down on the Dallas 13.

An incomplete pass, then a run brought the ball to the six, with just 58 seconds left. The next play was

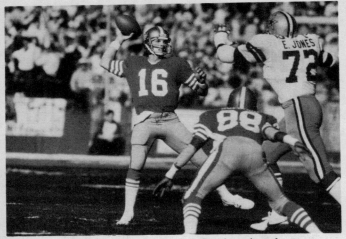

With 6′9″ Ed "Too Tall" Jones (72) bearing down, a retreating Joe Montana (16) gets set to throw the winning TD toss to end Dwight Clark during San Francisco's NFC title game victory over Dallas in 1981.

designed to go to Solomon on the left side of the end zone. But when Joe looked for him, he was covered. With the Dallas defenders closing in, Joe sprinted out to the right, looking for Dwight Clark. Clark was trying to shake his defender at the rear of the end zone.

With 6-foot-9 Ed "Too Tall" Jones bearing down on him, Joe waited, moving backward. When he saw the opening, he threw, off the wrong foot and moving backward. The ball floated high toward the rear of the end zone to clear the outstretched hands of the defenders. The question was, would it clear Clark's hands, too?

But at the last instant Clark leaped high in the air

and made a brilliant catch of a brilliant throw. Touchdown! The 'Niners had scored. Ray Wersching's kick made it a 28–27 game, and when the defense held Dallas for the remaining seconds, the 'Niners had won it.

Montana's throw and Clark's catch made the highlight films all around the country. The play still makes the highlight films. It was the Comeback Kid at his best, a great moment in the history of the San Francisco franchise. The Niners went on to win the Super Bowl that year, whipping Cincinnati, 26–21, and Joe Montana was named Most Valuable Player.

Montana and the 'Niners repeated their Super success three years later, whipping the Dolphins in the big one. By that time, Joe Montana was considered the premier quarterback in pro football. But as good as he is, he's most dangerous when his team is behind and time is running out. And just when it looks like his team can't possibly win—Boom! It's the Comeback Kid. And that's when the great moments really come.

A Milestone for the Juice

There were times when it seemed that every time O.J. Simpson carried the football, he was setting some kind of record or creating a great moment. This was especially true during his two seasons at the University of Southern California in 1967 and '68. During that time, Orenthel James Simpson became perhaps the most recognizable athlete in America.

Even fans who followed mainly the pro game and not college ball knew when USC was playing and asked the question that became standard fare for football fans everywhere.

"How many yards did O.J. get today?"

He certainly had all the tools. The 6-foot-2, 205-pound halfback could run the hundred in 9.4 seconds, cut on a dime, and break away from the strongest of tacklers. In addition, he had that sometimes undefinable quality known as charisma. Week after week, his legend grew.

His junior year at USC, 1967 (he was a junior college transfer), resulted in 1,543 yards on 291 carries and 13 touchdowns. The next year he gained 1,880 yards on an unbelievable 383 carries and scored 23 times. His yardage total was a single-season record for major colleges to that time. And when the season ended, he was awarded the Heisman Trophy as the best college player in the land.

By now, football fans were salivating over the prospects of O.J. playing in the National Football League. He seemed like a once-in-a-generation runner who would have the chance to break all the rushing records in the book. O.J. would have dearly loved to remain on the west coast, but he had to follow NFL rules, and it must have been a disappointment when he was drafted by the Buffalo Bills.

He had been the NFL's first pick, but he'd be going to a team that had a miserable 1-12-1 record the year before. And when he finally signed and began to play, he found himself operating behind a weak offensive line aptly nicknamed "The Vanishing Five."

No running back can gain big yards without good blocking. The linemen must open some kind of holes to get the back started. For three years at Buffalo, O.J. paid the price. He gained 697, 488, and 742 yards, a far cry from USC days. No longer were fans asking that weekly question: "How many yards did O.J. get?"

Some thought O.J. would try to leave Buffalo after

1972, when his initial contract was up. But he surprised everyone by remaining. One reason was that in 1972 the Bills had brought back a former coach, Lou Saban, who had always built winners in the past. Saban was quick to announce that his offense at Buffalo would be built around the running of O.J. Simpson. That was all the Juice had to hear.

Saban was true to his word, and despite numerous injuries on the offensive line, the Juice started looking like the O.J. of old. When the season ended, he was atop the NFL's rushes with 1,251 yards on 292 carries. And he had impressed a lot of people.

"We lost five guards, a center, and a tackle during the course of the year," said Bills' publicist Don Phinney. "So O.J. had to be constantly making adjustments. He would have had 1,500 yards if it weren't for the injuries. I can't begin to tell you how many yards he made on his own.

With the Bills improving, would 1,500 yards be a realistic goal for 1973? Coming into training camp that year, O.J. upgraded even that prediction. He told his good friend, guard Reggie McKenzie, that he wanted to shoot for 1,700 yards in the upcoming season. McKenzie looked at his friend and said quickly:

"Why not make it an even two thousand!"

"Why not," O.J. replied, just as quickly.

Whether O.J. and McKenzie actually believed 2,000 was possible is hard to say. The NFL mark was 1,863 yards, set by the incomparable Jim Brown in 1963. Brown was almost universally acknowledged as the best running back ever, so his rushing record was set up on a pretty high pedestal. But when the Juice rambled for 250 yards in Buffalo's opener against New England, it was a foreshadowing of things to come.

Both O.J. and the Bills continued to play well during the first half of the season. By midseason, a revved up Simpson was over the 1,000-yard mark (1,025) and talk of a 2,000-yard season surfaced once again. It was no longer a pipe dream. If anyone could do it, O.J. Simpson could.

But then a couple of sub-par games took the Juice off his record course. Though he was still putting together a great season, anything short of a run at Brown's record and then 2,000 yards might be considered a disappointment. It came down to this. With two games remaining, he had gained 1,584 yards. He was 279 yards shy of Brown's mark. Getting that would be tough, but not impossible. But getting 416 yards to reach 2,000, well, that seemed too much to ask of any mortal running back.

Then came a rematch with New England. O.J. was simply spectacular all afternoon, reeling off one big gain after another. When the smoke cleared, he had gained 219 yards on 22 carries, averaging nearly ten yards a pop. What's more, he was now within 60 yards of Jim Brown's record and within 197 of 2,000. Things were getting interesting. The Bills would wind up the season playing the New York Jets at Shea Stadium in New York. Besides O.J.'s personal goals, there was also a playoff berth at stake.

It was a cold December 16 at Shea, and there was snow in the air. Even O.J. sensed the possible magnitude of his achievement. The night before the game he was especially restless, telling Reggie McKenzie, "I wish we could get this thing over with."

The Bills' offense took the field that day with two things in mind. First, they wanted to get O.J. the record, alleviate that pressure, then concentrate on winning the game. They had to win and hope that Houston could beat Cincinnati if they were to make the playoffs.

Juice showed he was primed and ready. On the second play from scrimmage he bolted around the right side and rambled for 30 yards. He might have broken the record right there if he hadn't slipped on the snowy field at the Jets' 34-yard line. But it was a good start anyway.

They continued to run O.J. at the Jets. Though it was obvious that the Bills wanted their popular star to get the record quickly, the Jets were nevertheless having trouble stopping the elusive number 32. Five plays later Simpson was within four yards of Jim Brown's mark.

The next time Buffalo got the ball, O.J. got the call. Once again he started circling the end. This time the Jets closed in, but not before O.J. had gained six yards. That was enough. He had set a new, single-season rushing mark and the Jets fans cheered the great moment that had unfolded before them.

"We tried everything to stop him and it didn't work,"

Jets' linebacker Paul Crane said later. "They came to get the record for him and they did."

Now, it was back to business. The record might have been his, but the game still had to be won. So O.J. continued to ramble. Before the half ended, he ran 13 yards for another Buffalo score, and a short time later a punt return gave the Bills still another.

Moments after the run that gave him a record-breaking 2,003 yards, the great O. J. Simpson is given the game ball by the official.

It was a 21–7 game at the half, and when the stats came down it was learned that the Juice was up to 1,910 yards. With 30 minutes of football left, the magical 2,000 was a real possibility. So once again the Juice began getting the football. He gained three, lost three, gained eight. It wasn't coming easy. Finally he ripped off a 25-yarder. That brought him within 50 yards of the next plateau.

The offensive line, which had worked so hard for the Juice all year, looked for a second wind to make that final push. The snow was falling now, the footing becoming slippery. But O.J. Simpson kept carrying the football. He ran for eight, then 22, then nine, then five more. He was now at 1,997 yards and still some six minutes remained in the game.

Quarterback Joe Ferguson then gave the ball to O.J. for the 34th time, and the Juice bolted through a hole opened by Reggie McKenzie and ripped off a solid seven-yard gain. That did it. His total was now 2,003 yards, a magical mark and momentous achievement. O.J. then left the field to a standing ovation.

It was a great day for O.J. Simpson, one of the greatest ever. Not only had he become the first man in pro football history to gain more than 2,000 yards in a season, but he finished that final game with 200 yards on 34 carries. It was his third 200-yard game of the year, still another record.

Believe it or not, O.J.'s record lasted about as long as Brown's. In 1984, the Rams' Eric Dickerson set a new standard of 2,105 yards, while in the upstart United

States Football League, Herschel Walker broke Dickerson's record. The difference was games played. Jim Brown set his mark over a 14-game schedule. O.J. did it in 14, Dickerson in 16, and Walker in 18.

Yet all are great runners and each produced a super season. And while each record represents a great moment in itself, no one who witnessed it will ever forget the sight of O.J. Simpson churning through the snow of Shea Stadium in pursuit of a dream. That may have been the greatest rushing moment of them all.

Walter's Biggest Day

In some ways Walter Payton is a walking great moment. The rugged halfback of the Chicago Bears has been playing at an all-pro level since his rookie year of 1975. And he shows no signs of slowing down. In 1985, at the age of 31, Walter Payton gained 1,551 yards on 324 carries. That's a lot of running, even for a much younger man.

But Walter, who has always taken meticulous care of his body and kept himself in marvelous shape, gave no evidence of Father Time gaining on him. By 1985 he was the National Football League's all-time leading ground gainer, with 14,860 yards at season's end. And to show his continuing durability, Walter set another mark in '85 by gaining 100 yards or more in nine consecutive games.

The Walter Payton story can go on and on. For instance, after years of playing with mediocre Bears teams, Walter was finally rewarded in '85 when the Chicagoans emerged as the best team in the entire NFL, losing only one game during the regular season and going on to win the Super Bowl with a one-sided victory over the New England Patriots.

And as he has done since day one, the 5-foot-10½, 205-pounder with a body etched in granite, played an integral part in his team's success. That success had been predicted ever since Walter Payton was drafted number one out of Jackson State in 1975. When the Bears backfield coach back then, Fred O'Connor, saw young Walter stripped to the waist, he made a comment which is remembered to this day. "When I saw Walter for the first time," O'Connor said, "I thought to myself that God must have taken a chisel and said, 'I'm gonna make me a halfback.'"

But of all Walter's great days on the gridiron, perhaps his greatest came back in 1977, his third year with the Bears. As usual, the team was struggling. After nine games that year, the club had a 4–5 record. If they wanted to make the playoffs, the Chicagoans would have to start winning now.

Walter was in the midst of his greatest season to date. After nine games he already had 1,129 yards and looked as if he might have an outside shot at O.J. Simpson's mark of 2,003 yards for a season. Game ten that year was against NFC Central rival Minnesota. The Vikes were leading the division and whenever the two clubs met, the game was usually tough and hard-hitting.

As the Bears got ready for the game with the Vikes, there was some bad news. Walter Payton was down with a bad case of the flu. He was only practicing lightly and didn't know how much he'd be able to play on Sunday. There was even some talk about holding him out of the game unless he was really needed. On game day Walter felt weak as he left the locker room and headed out toward the field.

"I was having hot and cold flashes," he recalled, later, "and I didn't really think I could put on a Walter Payton performance."

But Walter wasn't about to miss a big game with the Vikings. When the Chicago offense came on the field for the first time, Walter was right there with them. And on the first play from scrimmage, quarterback Bob Avellini decided to find out just how much his halfback had to give. He called a sweep, and with the blocking to get him started, Walter rambled for 29 yards. He bounced right up and trotted back to the huddle. A good sign.

Avellini continued to call Walter's number and get results, though the game remained scoreless through the first period. Midway through the second, a shanked punt gave the Bears the football on the Viking 23. From the 15, Walter carried four straight times for the score. The kick made it a 7–0 game.

Now the Bears were really calling on their star runner. He got six, then 23, then 11 yards. A short time later he rambled for 14, then 27 more, as well as several shorter runs. A Bob Thomas field goal made it 10–0 late in the period, and that was still the score at the half. But even more surprising were the halftime stats. They showed that Walter Payton had already gained 144 yards, a total considered outstanding for an entire game. And he was supposed to be ill with the flu!

The Vikings got a score early in the third period to bring the count to 10–7. As usual, the two teams were in a close, rock-ribbed game. So the Bears went to their best weapon. They gave the ball to Walter Payton even more, and he continued to respond. He was going right and left, and up the middle, using his great moves and his strength to break tackles. His running ate up the clock and enabled the Bears to hold to their slim, 10–7 lead.

Now, with just minutes left, Walter had gained 210 yards, his best effort as a pro. He had already carried the ball 37 times and could have called it a day. But his team still needed him to eat up the clock and keep the Vikings from putting their offense on the field.

The ball was at the Chicago 33 when Walter got it once more. There was a pile-up at the line, so Walter shifted gears, glided smoothly to his right, then hurdled over several tangled bodies and broke into the clear. By the time he was bumped out of bounds at the nine-yard line he had gained 58 yards, putting his total at 268 for the day!

Until the 58-yard burst, incredible in itself considering Walter's pregame physical condition and the fact that it was his 38th carry of the day, no one had given too much thought about the single game rushing mark.

But suddenly Walter was knocking at the door, just five yards away from the 273 yards gained by the great O.J. Simpson just a year earlier. But the long run had made everyone acutely aware of the situation. The Vikings, the Bears, and all those watching knew that Walter Payton would get the ball again.

On the next play he swept to the left side and plowed ahead for three yards. That brought him to 271, two away from the record. With the final seconds ticking away, Walter got the call for the 40th time. Once again the Viking defenders grabbed and clutched at him. But somehow, he managed to find the strength to drag three Vikes with him to the two. The gain of four gave him 275 yards on the day. He had set a new mark! And with that, the gun sounded. The Bears had also won the game, 10–7.

It was difficult not to marvel at Walter Payton's record-breaking performance. He poured it on all game long against a bruising Viking defense that hated to yield to anyone. And despite having the flu most of the week he looked amazingly fresh after his 40th carry.

"If the game had gone into overtime," Walter said, "I imagine I could have gone some more. I felt weak during the introductions and there were times I had to suck it in and go extra hard. But I seemed to get stronger as we wore the Vikings down."

It seemed as if nothing could wear Walter Payton down in 1977. Going into the final game with the Giants, Walter had 1,805 yards. Another 200-yard game would enable him to break Simpson's mark of 2,003.

Walter Payton looks upfield, ready to turn the corner en route to an incredible 275-yard record-setting day against the Vikings in 1977.

There were many people who thought Walter could do it. But that's when fate took a hand.

On game day the field at the Meadowlands in New Jersey was an icy, slushy mess. None of the players could really get their footing, and Walter managed just a sloppy, tough 47 yards. Yet it was his catch of an Avellini pass that brought the ball from the New York Giants 25 to the 11 that enabled Bob Thomas to kick the field goal that gave Chicago the win, 12–9 in overtime, and put them in the playoffs. Payton can beat you so many ways.

"The win was the most important thing to Walter," said fullback Roland Harper, after the game. "He knew we needed it and it was a matter of first things first. The record didn't mean anything to him."

That statement captures the essence of the man they call "Sweetness". His team has always come before individual glory. He finished with 1,852 yards, third best season total up to that time. But despite being a team man, Walter has given fans many great moments en route to becoming the league's all-time ground-gaining champion. It just couldn't happen any other way.

The Most Famous
Guaranteed Win Ever

To some, this one was the greatest moment of them all. Of course, if you were rooting for the other team . . . then you've probably spent nearly twenty years trying to forget it. The time was January 12, 1969, and the event the Super Bowl. This was only the third meeting between the American Football League and National Football League champions, and Vince Lombardi's NFL Green Bay Packers had won the first two with relative ease.

When the Baltimore Colts became the NFL representative in Super Bowl III, no one figured anything would change. After all, the Colts had lost only one game all year, a 30–20 defeat by Cleveland. They avenged that by whipping the Browns, 34–0, in the playoffs to win the NFL crown. Coach Don Shula had a powerful team on both offense and defense, a worthy successor to Lombardi's Packers.

The AFL would be represented by its third different team in three years. Both the Kansas City Chiefs and the Oakland Raiders had fallen far short in their battles against Green Bay; now the New York Jets would take up the AFL banner against the Colts. The AFL, however, had only been in existence since 1960, and despite the pending merger between the two leagues, most experts still felt National Football League football was far superior to that played in the AFL. Thus, as Super Bowl III approached, the Colts were made overwhelming favorites, the early spread giving them an 18- to 23-point advantage.

But the Jets were not about to roll over and hand the game to the Colts. For one thing, the New Yorkers were coached by Weeb Ewbank, who had been the Colts' mentor in the famous 1958 NFL overtime title win against the New York Giants. So Ewbank would be going up against his former team, giving his players an added incentive, to win it for the popular coach.

New York had lost only three games during the regular AFL season and had whipped tough Oakland, 27–23, to get into the super game. The club was considered solid on both offense and defense, though most figured they just weren't in the same class with the Colts. One Jet player who disagreed quite vocally was the Jets' quarterback, Joe Namath, the American Football League's Most Valuable Player in 1968.

It didn't surprise too many people to find Namath in the middle of the pregame controversy. He had been a highly visible and vocal athlete since his days at the

University of Alabama under Coach Bear Bryant. At Alabama, Namath really made national headlines at the Orange Bowl in January of 1965. Relegated to the bench by a knee injury, the senior quarterback watched the top-ranked Crimson Tide fall behind Texas, 14–0.

By the middle of the second quarter, Coach Bryant had no choice. He sent in Namath, his knee heavily bandaged, and Joe Willie put on a courageous show, passing for 255 yards and bringing the Tide within inches of victory. With the score 21–17 in the final session, Namath tried to sneak the ball in from the one. The Longhorns held and then ran out the clock to win.

Yet his performance had convinced everyone of his courage and his talent, and when the New York Jets of the young American Football League drafted him, they were determined to sign him. A player with Namath's charisma and talent could give the league instant respectability. That's when Joe got his now famous $400,000 contract, the biggest ever up to that time, and brought his act to New York.

Once there, he continued to make headlines, whether it be with a Fu Manchu mustache, his white shoes, or the many different ladies he squired around town. That brought about his nickname, Broadway Joe Namath.

Yet during it all he was an improving quarterback with an improving team. He was poised, intelligent, had a cannon for an arm, and had one of the quickest releases in the business. The only drawback were his

89

knees, which became a constant problem. But when they were sound, he was one of the best. And they were sound for Super Bowl III.

It didn't take long for Namath to mouth off. The Colts were quarterbacked by veteran Earl Morrall, who had taken over for the legendary, but injured John Unitas. Morrall tossed for 26 TD passes and was named the NFL's Most Valuable Player, but that didn't stop Joe Namath from taking pot shots.

He said there were at least five quarterbacks in the AFL better than Morrall. "I study quarterbacks," he added, "and I assure you the Colts haven't had to go against quarterbacks like we have in the AFL."

That started it. The Colts were incensed. How dare Namath talk like that about their leader, especially when he and his teammates were still 17-point underdogs. That's still the largest pregame point spread of any Super Bowl before or since. The verbal exchanges continued almost to game time. That's when Namath came out with one of the most widely known quotes in all of sports. Asked one more time about the outcome of the game, Namath said, "The Jets will win on Sunday. Not only do I think it, but I guarantee it!"

To many, that was the kiss of death. Namath had given the Colts more than enough ammunition to be sky high for the game, which would be played on that same Orange Bowl field where Namath had been so great as a collegian. For the first few minutes it looked as if the predictions were right. The Jets gained some yards on the ground, but were forced to punt.

The Colts took over on their own 27, and Earl Morrall wasted no time moving his team. A screen pass to tight end John Mackey gained 19 yards. Running back Tom Matte rambled for ten. Three more carries by the backs netted another first down. Then a pass to Tom Mitchell gained 15 more, and the Colts had a first down on the Jets' 19. It was going about as everyone expected.

A quick score here would probably signal the beginning of a rout. But suddenly things went sour. A dropped pass, an overthrown pass, then a sack of Morrall by middle linebacker Al Atkinson and the Colts were forced to try a 27-yard field goal. The kick by veteran Lou Michaels went wide. The Jets had held!

Before long, the Jets were playing the Colts very tough. It was a ballgame, and the veteran Colt players knew it. Even the fans at the Orange Bowl and the millions watching on TV wondered when the Jets would crack. Or better yet, *if* they would crack.

The Colts missed another golden opportunity late in the first period, as one of Morrall's passes was intercepted in the end zone, so the young Jets got still another shot in the arm. Despite Namath's boasts, the Jets still had to prove they could play with the Colts, and during the first quarter, they had.

After the interception, the complexion of the game began to change. The Jets got the ball at their own 20 and began taking it right at the heart of the Colts defense. With each play, the New York offensive line seemed to grow in confidence. They began to realize they could handle the Colts, and before long fullback

Matt Snell was ripping off big gains, and hurting people as he ran. At the same time, Namath began mixing his plays, throwing to his backs and wide receivers, especially George Sauer, Jr.

The quarterback with the big mouth was backing it up with his quick arm and agile football mind. He hit Sauer for 14 and 11 yards. After a two-yard gain by halfback Emerson Boozer, Namath tossed to Snell for 12 more and first down at the Baltimore nine. It took just two plays for the big fullback to smash into the end zone for the game's first score. Jim Turner's conversion made it a 7–0 game. Could it be that the impossible was beginning to happen?

It was the Jets defense that took over and dominated the remainder of the first half. Whenever the Colts threatened, the defense came up with the big play. A 58-yard run by Tom Matte brought the ball to the Jets' 16. Two plays later from the 15, Morall dropped back and fired toward Willie Richardson at the goal line. But Johnny Sample, a former Colt, made a key interception to stop the drive.

Minutes later, the Colts got the ball back and tried the old flea flicker play. Quarterback Morrall had receiver Jimmy Orr wide open near the goal line, but didn't see him. When he tried to go to fullback Jerry Hill instead, safety Jim Hudson intercepted for the Jets once more. At halftime, it was still a 7–0 game and thoughts of a Colt rout were being pushed into the background. Now it was more a question of whether the Colts could win the game at all.

Super Bowl III provided football's greatest upset. One reason why was the protection given New York Jets quarterback Joe Namath. Broadway Joe had many moments like this, time to look downfield and pick apart the Baltimore defense as the Jets won, 17–6.

If the beginning of the second half was any indication, they couldn't. Tom Matte fumbled on the first play from scrimmage and the Jets recovered. Nine plays later, Jim Turner booted a 32-yard field goal and the New Yorkers had a 10–0 lead. A short time later, Turner was at it again. His 30-yard field goal upped the lead to 13–0.

Finally Baltimore turned to its legendary quarterback, veteran John Unitas, who had been the big hero ten years earlier against the Giants. Still nursing a sore elbow, Unitas was only at about 80 percent, but wanted to play. Maybe Johnny U's charismatic magic would rub off on his teammates and they would rally.

But on this day Unitas couldn't pull off any miracles. Another Turner field goal made it 16–0, and by the time Johnny U got the Colts on the board, it was too late. The final score was 16–7 in perhaps the greatest gridiron upset of all time.

Though it wasn't a gigantic score, the Jets had dominated the entire game. Namath hit on 17 of 28 passes for 206 yards, eight of them going to George Sauer for 133 yards. He threw only when necessary, since fullback Snell was chewing up the Colts with 30 carries for 121 yards. In addition to controlling the ball, the Jets intercepted four Colt passes to blunt potential scoring drives. No doubt about it, the American Football League had arrived!

After the game, there was no more bragging from Joe Namath. He was a pro, as were the Colts, and he wasn't about to rub salt on their wounds. He said he didn't intend to put the rap on the Colts beforehand.

"There was never any question in my mind that we could move against their defense," he said. "And what I said about Earl Morrall wasn't intended as a rap. It was only meant as a statement of fact."

Then Joe summed up the entire game that had shocked a nation, put the Jets, Namath, and the American Football League on the map, and shamed the older NFL with an ignominious defeat. Said Broadway Joe:

"We didn't win on passing or running, or on defense. We beat them in every phase of the game."

The Grace of a Swann

He had the perfect name for a wide receiver. Lynn Swann. A receiver who would glide and float, leap and soar like a ballet dancer. Lynn Swann. He could run and cut, catch them short or catch them deep, and he was a threat to score from any place on the field.

Of course, Lynn Swann is no secret to football fans. He was the all-pro wide receiver of the Pittsburgh Steelers who teamed with Terry Bradshaw, Franco Harris, Rocky Bleier, and John Stallworth to form the heart of the Steeler offense that helped the club win four Super Bowls between 1975 and 1980.

Grace and pure athletic ability were always hall-marks of Lynn Swann's career, from the time he came out of the University of Southern California as an all-American wide receiver right up to his retirement while still in his prime. He always did things with class and did it well.

The 6-foot, 180-pound Swann's penchant for coming up with the big game was no accident. He produced great moments because he geared himself to do it. As Swann himself once said:

"The key to my success is the homework I do before a game. There are a lot of talented guys in the league, receivers with great ability. It's the preparation they do that sets them apart. You have to know just what to do with all that talent when you take it on the field."

But perhaps of all the great moments that highlighted Lynn Swann's career, the greatest occurred in just his second year in the NFL. And it couldn't have occurred in a better place: at the Super Bowl, football's most glamorous and visible showcase.

Both Swann and John Stallworth were Steeler rookies in 1974. And while they were to become the game's most devastating pass-catching duo, Steeler Coach Chuck Noll broke them in slowly that first year. Lynn caught only 11 passes for 208 yards and two scores that first year. But his 18.9 yards per catch established him as a bona fide deep threat and his 14.1 average returning 41 punts led the league. There was little doubt about his ultimate ability.

There was one big thrill before Lynn's rookie year ended. The Steelers won the Super Bowl, defeating the Minnesota Vikings, 16–10. Lynn didn't catch a pass in the big one, but averaged 11.3 yards on punt returns, a Super Bowl record.

It was a thrill to be on a Super Bowl winner as a rookie, but Lynn continued to work and the next year became a starter, and not long afterward, a star. With the Steelers taking another AFC Central Division title with a 12–2 mark. Lynn Swann was a big contributor with 49 catches for 781 yards and a conference leading 11 touchdowns. In his second year he had become an all-pro.

The 1975 playoffs started with an easy win over Baltimore. The Steelers prevailed, 28–10, and now would face always-tough Oakland for the AFC title. It was a bruising battle between two great teams. Though the Steelers won, 16–10, to advance to the Super Bowl once again, the victory was not without a price.

In the third period, Swann went after a Bradshaw pass over the middle and was hit high and hard by safety George Atkinson. When he tried to get up, he collapsed and had to be carried from the field. He was in the hospital for two nights under observation. The doctors knew he had a concussion, but wanted to make sure there was nothing more.

Now the question. Would Lynn be recovered enough to play in the Super Bowl? Fortunately, there is a two-week break between the conference championships and the big game. So there might be enough time. The Steelers would be meeting another great team, the Dallas Cowboys, and they really needed the talents of Lynn Swann to be at full strength.

Lynn stayed away from workouts for a week, and when he returned he still wasn't going all out in full contact practice. The questions were many, and his answers cautious.

"You don't go through 23 games in a season just to miss out on the Super Bowl," he said. "But even the Super Bowl isn't as important as your health and your life. I kind of value that more than one football game."

Statements such as that made people wonder all over again. But when the doctors gave him full medical clearance, Lynn declared himself ready. Immediately some of the Cowboy defenders began openly questioning Lynn, whether he would go full tilt or worry about absorbing another blow to the head.

"I thought about it," Lynn admitted, just before the game. "But finally I just said the heck with it. I'm going out there and playing 100 percent. Any NFL player who thinks about his last injury is washed up. The Cowboys obviously don't know Lynn Swann and they don't know the Pittsburgh Steelers."

So Swann was ready as he took the field at the Orange Bowl in Miami in front of more than 75,000 fans and millions more on television. In fact, there was no one, including perhaps Lynn himself, who knew just how ready he was.

It was the Cowboys who drew first blood, recovering a fumble by the Pittsburgh punter at the Steeler 29. On the first play from scrimmage, Roger Staubach hit Drew Pearson over the middle and the receiver raced into the end zone for the score. The kick made it 7–0, and the game wasn't yet five minutes old.

Like any great champion, the Steelers were sometimes most dangerous when behind, and it didn't take them long to come storming back. Starting at the

The incredibly acrobatic Lynn Swann makes one of his circus catches against the Dallas Cowboys in Super Bowl X. Swann was the game's MVP as the Steelers went on to win it all.

Dallas 33, Franco Harris and Rocky Bleier ran the ball to the Cowboy 48. Then Terry Bradshaw dropped back, looking for Lynn. He fired it deep down the right side. But it looked as if the pass was sailing high and would go out of bounds incomplete.

But at the last second Swann leaped high in the air, much higher than his defender, and caught the ball. Then he somehow twisted his body in midair and managed to come down in bounds at the 16. It was an incredible catch, a 32-yard gain, and put the Steelers into scoring position. Several plays later, Bradshaw hit tight end Randy Grossman for the score, and the kick made it a 7–7 ballgame.

"That catch seemed to boost me up," Swann said later. "After that, I never had a day in my life when I felt so loose."

Dallas took a 10–7 lead in the second period, and while the Steelers didn't score, Swann gave the fans another great moment. Bradshaw went deep down the middle and Lynn ran under the ball along with a Dallas defender. Somehow Swann got his hands on it, juggled it, and then grabbed it again as he was falling for an unbelievable, 53-yard gain. Unfortunately, the Steelers couldn't convert, and the Cowboys took a 10–7 lead into the lockerroom at halftime.

After a scoreless third period, the Steelers seemed to be in trouble. The Dallas defense was shutting them down. But at the start of the final session, Pittsburgh forced a safety to make it a 10–9 game. Then a 26-yard field goal made it 12–10, with less than half the quarter remaining. An interception led to still another field goal, giving Pittsburgh a 15–10 lead. But the Cowboys were just a touchdown from the lead, so the Steelers wanted more.

They had the ball at their own 36. It was a third and four, and the Cowboys looked for the run, or the short pass for the first. Bradshaw had other ideas. He dropped back and looked deep downfield. There was a streaking Lynn Swann, letting it all out, and Bradshaw cranked up his powerful arm. He fired a bullet out deep and Swann ran under it, catching it two strides behind the defender and racing all the way to the end zone. It was a 64-yard scoring play, and while the extra point was missed, it still gave the Steelers a 21–10 cushion.

Dallas made it interesting. A touchdown pass by Staubach brought the score to 21–17, and the Steel Curtain defense had to stop the Jolly Roger once more before the victory was sealed. And when it was over, the game's Most Valuable Player was none other than Lynn Swann.

He had been simply magnificent. Sandwiched between his three great catches was an 12-yard reception that gave him four catches on the day for an amazing 161 yards. Two of the catches were acrobatic classics, and the TD grab was an electrifying, gamebreaking play. Swann had truly given the fans a great moment to remember. And what's more, he had come out of a hospital bed to do it. That kind of production under adverse circumstances is the real mark of a superstar. And Lynn Swann was a superstar of the first magnitude.

101

The Grit and Toughness of Kellen Winslow

There was a time when a 6-foot-5, 250-pound football player had to be an interior lineman, a guard or tackle, or a center. But no more. In today's game, many of the linemen approach 300 pounds and the 250-pounders are linebackers and occasionally even fullbacks. And a few are tight ends.

But there was one 250-pound tight end who completely revolutionized the position when he joined the San Diego Chargers in 1979. Despite his great size, Kellen Winslow was fast, agile, and could catch the football. As soon as he became familiar with Coach Don Coryell's pass-oriented offense, Winslow began catching Dan Fouts' aerials like no tight end before him.

A broken leg in the seventh game of his rookie season slowed his progress. At that time he had a team-leading 25 catches for 255 yards and a pair of scores.

But it was in the 1980 season that Kellen Winslow really blossomed. He grabbed an NFL leading 89 passes, most ever by a tight end, and they were good for 1,290 yards and nine touchdowns. He also averaged 14.5 yards a catch, exceptionally good for a tight end. He was already rewriting the book.

The next season he proved it was no fluke. Once again Kellen Winslow led the NFL with 88 receptions, this time for 1,075 yards and ten scores. He was all-pro once again and already being talked about as possibly the best tight end ever. But it wasn't easy for him.

"It seems to be getting more physical out there," he said. "The more balls I catch the harder they seem to try to hit me. Sometimes it gets a bit ridiculous. I'd catch a pass, go down, and guys would be flying over the pile trying to get a piece of me."

Yet Kellen couldn't be intimidated. And when the Chargers finished the 1981 season with a 10–6 record to take the AFC West crown, they were in the playoffs. In the first round they would be traveling to the Orange Bowl to meet the Miami Dolphins. It was destined to be a game of great moments, with the greatest provided by the play of Kellen Winslow.

It didn't start as if it were going to be a great game. Instead, it began as a rout. Before the first quarter had ended, the Chargers had a 24–0 lead and seemed to have the game locked up. But in the second period, the Dolphins switched to backup quarterback Don Strock. He had the hot hand and by halftime had brought the Dolphins back to within seven, at 24–17.

When Strock hit tight end Joe Rose with a 15-yard scoring pass early in the third period, the game was suddenly tied. And at this point, it was to become a classic. As the Chargers began driving again, quarterback Fouts was looking more and more to Kellen Winslow. Despite a sore shoulder and a constant battering by the Miami defense, Kellen continued to get free and catch passes.

From the Miami 25, Fouts dropped back and found Kellen in the end zone for the go-ahead score. But before the period ended, Strock had thrown for a TD of his own, and at the end of three quarters, the game was deadlocked, 31–31. Now the tension was as high as the heat and humidity in Miami's Orange Bowl. Fatigue was becoming a factor as the two teams continued to battle, looking for the break, or another shift in momentum.

Because of the battering he had taken, Kellen was suffering from dehydration, which led to severe cramps. Several times he had to be helped from the field. But after a minute or so on the sidelines he was right back in there.

It didn't look good when early in the final period, Miami intercepted a Fouts pass and marched in for a score. The kick made it 38–31, the Dolphins' first lead of the day. If the Chargers were going to fold, this would be the moment.

With time now running down, Miami drove again. Another score would just about do it. But Andra Franklin fumbled, and the Chargers recovered at their

It's another catch in heavy traffic for Kellen Winslow against Miami in the 1982 playoffs. The San Diego tight end was unstoppable all afternoon, despite being surrounded by defenders.

own 18. Fouts began driving his team once more. He hit Kellen with several passes during the drive, and each time he caught a ball, the big guy had to leave the field, at least for a play. Even the announcers calling the game thought he was through several times. But, incredibly, he kept coming back for more.

Finally, with the ball at the nine, Fouts hit James Brooks in the end zone for the score. Rolf Benirschke's kick tied the game at 38. There were now just 58 seconds left in regulation time.

But the Dolphins didn't want overtime. Strock completed several quick passes following the kickoff, and suddenly Uwe von Schamann was on to try a 43-yard field goal that could win it. Both teams dug in, ready to go all out for what could be the last play of the game.

The ball was snapped, placed down, and . . . It was blocked! The kick was blocked. Incredibly, big number 80 had leaped high in the air to get a hand on the kick as it left von Schamann's foot. Big number 80 was none other than Kellen Winslow. To this day, no one knows where he got the strength. He wasn't even expected to be in there. But as Coach Coryell said later:

"Kellen leaps higher than anyone on the team."

Now the game was in sudden-death overtime. With players on both teams nearly exhausted, the contest continued. The Chargers had the first shot at winning, but Benirschke missed a 27-yarder. Then the Dolphins drove, but left 75,000 broken hearts when von Schamann missed the game-winner, this time from 34 yards out. Then, with time running down in the first overtime period, the Chargers began to move once more.

But the drive looked ready to stall when San Diego came up with a third and 20 at their own 45. Fouts dropped back to pass once again. The receivers downfield were covered, so he flipped a short pass to Kellen in the left flat. Bone-weary with exhaustion and cramps, the big guy turned upfield. He was gaining good yardage, but the Miami defense began swarming around him. They grabbed at him, but he lowered his shoulder and plowed forward, despite several tacklers

Slammed to the ground again and again by two or three Miami defenders, Kellen Winslow kept catching passes. He had to be helped from the field several times, yet always returned to action to catch another pass.

now hanging on him. Somehow, he reached deep down for a last ounce of strength and lunged forward before he was finally buried.

Kellen didn't move. He lay on the Orange Bowl turf until his teammates helped him off the field. But he had done it. He had gained the 20 yards needed for the first down. And he did it with the most incredible show of second effort anyone had ever seen. Even the huge crowd at the Orange Bowl was stunned to silence by his dramatic, gut-wrenching run.

Several plays later, Benirschke was back on the field, and this time his 29-yard field goal try was good! The

Chargers had won it, 41–38, in one of the greatest games ever played. Fouts had set playoff records with 33 of 53 passes for 433 yards, while Strock had hit on 28 of 42 for 397 yards.

But it was Kellen Winslow who captured the admiration of friend and foe alike. The big guy had gathered in 13 passes for 166 yards. He had also blocked the potential winning field goal, and made his incredible last run to set up his team's winning score.

"I was proud to call myself Kellen's teammate today," said veteran receiver Charlie Joiner. "And I think everyone else agrees."

Kellen had left the field with a badly bruised shoulder, a cut lip, and cramps throughout his body. Later he told everyone just how exhausting the game had been.

"I thought I was dead," he said. "My shoulder was going numb every time I was hit, and the cramps were coming on every play. There's got to be an easier way to make a living." Then he deadpanned, "You've got to excuse me now. I've got to go back to the field to pick up my heart and soul."

Kellen Winslow may not really have left his heart and soul out there on the Orange Bowl turf. But he did leave something behind. He left a truly great moment, orchestrated by a performance that no one watching will ever forget.

The Monsters of the Midway—Super Bears at Last

They were the dominant team in the early days of the National Football League. Originally known as the Chicago Staleys when the team was first started by George Halas, the name was changed to Bears a few years later, and Bears it's been ever since.

When the NFL played its first championship game back in 1933, the Chicago Bears were there, beating the New York Giants, 23–21. The Bears in those days had the likes of Bronko Nagurski and Red Grange in their lineup, and they would be rarely without big-name stars down through the years.

But the biggest name was the Chicago franchise itself. By 1940, the Bears were affectionately known as the "Monsters of the Midway," and they proved it that year by completely overwhelming the Washington Redskins in the title game, 73–0, the most one-sided championship victory in NFL history.

Those were the Bears of Sid Luckman, George McAfee, Ken Kavanaugh and other stars who became heroes in the Windy City. The Bears were in four straight title games starting in 1940, as George "Papa Bear" Halas, the owner-coach, shaped the personality of his club that has stood till this day. The Bears played a rough, hard-nosed brand of football, usually featuring a rock-ribbed defense that yielded ground grudgingly.

That could easily describe the 1963 version of the Bears, which ran up an 11–1–2 record in the regular season to edge the Green Bay Packers for the NFL West Crown. In the title game that year, the Bears whipped the Giants, 14–0, and the city of Chicago celebrated still another championship. They had a powerful team to root for, a team they felt would be right in the thick of things for years to come.

Yet despite the coming of new superstars like linebacker Dick Butkus and halfback Gale Sayers, the Bears could not regain the top spot. In fact, the fans of Chicago should have savored their title in 1963. Little did they know then, but there wouldn't be another one for more than 20 years.

As the team struggled to regain its identity in the 1970s, aging owner George Halas knew he had to do something. He had been with his beloved team since its inception in 1920, been there through all the championships, the good times and bad. But Halas could never tolerate the bad times. He wanted the old Bears back in the worst way. In 1982, shortly before his death at the age of 88, George "Papa Bear" Halas named Mike Ditka the team's new head coach.

Ditka. The name sounded like a Bear, in the same tradition of Nagurski and Butkus. And, indeed, he was. Ditka had been a tight end with the Bears during their final title season of 1963. He became an all-pro performer his first season and went on to a great career. Like the Bears of old, Dikta was a hard-nosed player who would take on a stone wall if he thought it would help win a ballgame.

He was an assistant coach with the Dallas Cowboys when Halas tabbed him to take over the Bears. It was an opportunity Ditka had always wanted. Halas wanted to bring back a mood, a feeling, the old aura of toughness that had always surrounded the Bears. And Ditka was the perfect man to do it.

Fortunately, he had the horses to work with. The Bears had a nucleus of fine, young players, and it didn't take them long to adapt themselves to the Ditka style. Working with defensive coordinator Buddy Ryan, Ditka molded a bruising, intimidating, hard-hitting defense that seemed to start coming of age late in 1984. They would put it all together in '85.

The offense was also in good hands, starting with running back Walter Payton, who in 1984 became the NFL's all-time leading rusher and, despite his 31 years, showed no signs of slowing down. Jim McMahon was a young, brash, gambling quarterback, who was a "gamer"—a player who perhaps didn't have the size, strength, and rocket arm of other QB's in the league, but made up for it with his daring, and the temperament of a gunfighter. When the game was on the line, his teammates knew McMahon would come through for them.

There were good receivers, including world-class sprinter Willie Gault, and a massive offensive line that loved pushing people around. The Bears made the playoffs in 1984, but lost in the NFC title game to eventual Super Bowl winner San Francisco, 23–0. So when 1985 rolled around, the Bears felt they had plenty to prove. And this was the year.

The season began on a high note. The team whipped the Tampa Bay Bucs, 38–28, and showed a lot of character in doing it. The Bucs had a 28–17 halftime lead, but the Chicago defense clamped down on their opponents in the final two sessions and the offense put 21 points on the board. McMahon tossed a pair of TDs and ran for two more, while Payton showed he still had his old verve with 120 yards on 17 carries.

That started it. In the ensuing weeks, the Chicagoans defeated New England, Minnesota, Washington, Tampa Bay again, and then San Francisco, the defending Super Bowl champs. The Bears won that one, 26–10, with the defense sacking all-pro quarterback Joe Montana seven times.

The roll continued, and the defense of Buddy Ryan was beginning to really dominate. Green Bay was beaten, 23–7; Minnesota lost, 27–9; the Packers were defeated again, 16–10; then Detroit fell, 24–3. Following those wins, the defense pitched a pair of shutouts, as the

Bears toppled Dallas, 44–0; and Atlanta, 36–0. In the Atlanta game, Payton tied an NFL record by rushing for 100 yards or more in his seventh straight game.

By now there was no doubt about it. The Bears were the best team in football. They had won twelve straight games, and there was talk of an undefeated season. In addition, the team was molding a distinct personality of its own, much like that of the old Bears, and with a definitely colorful cast of characters.

Payton, of course, was the best known of the Bears. But quarterback McMahon was also forging his own identity, with his omnipresent dark glasses (necessary because of a childhood eye injury, he said), his punk rock image, and his cockiness. They were the acknowledged leaders of the offense.

The defense was becoming even more well known. Defensive end Richard Dent was being called the best at his position, and the other end, Dan Hampton, wasn't that far behind. Middle linebacker Mike Singletary was being compared with the legendary Dick Butkus, and safety Gary Fencik was known for two things—being a graduate of Yale University and for hitting as hard as any safety in the game.

Then there was "The Refrigerator". William Perry was the team's number one draft choice out of Clemson, a 308-plus pound defensive tackle who caused all kinds of flak when he reported to camp far overweight. But he trimmed down and won a starting tackle job. He wasn't an all-pro, but he was an improving young player with a great future.

113

Yet it was his enormous appetite which led to his nickname and helped make him one of the most visible athletes in the country. And when Coach Ditka began using him on offense in goal-line situations, he got even more publicity. Soon everyone knew who The Refrigerator was.

In game 13, the Chicago express was finally derailed. The Miami Dolphins got hot early, taking a 31–10 halftime lead and coasting to a 38–24 victory, ending the Bears' hopes for an unbeaten year. But that was to be the only blemish. The team won its final three games to finish the year with a 15–1 mark and the NFC Central title. Now they were favorites in the playoffs.

That's when the great defense really rose to the occasion. Playing an explosive New York Giants team, the Bears shut them out, 21–0. Then came the NFC title game with the Los Angeles Rams. Once again the Chicago defense yielded nothing, except a lot of bruises and humiliation. They whipped the Rams, 24–0, becoming the first team to pitch back-to-back shutouts in the playoffs.

Now it was on to the Super Bowl. And to a man, the Bears were not satisfied with the achievement of getting there. They wanted to win, felt they had to win. They were the team of destiny, and they owed it to George Halas and all those great Bears teams of the past.

In Super Bowl XX, the Bears would be meeting another first-time Super Bowl team, the New England Patriots. The Pats, under Coach Raymond Berry, a Hall

This is a sight familiar to Chicago Bears fans. A host of Bears defenders sacking New England quarterback Tony Eason. This play came in Super Bowl XX, but the Chicago defense was doing it all year.

of Fame wide receiver who had teamed with John Unitas to form one of the great passing combos in history, had surprised the football world and finished the regular season with an 11–5 record.

During the regular season, the Pats led the AFC with 47 takeaways of turnovers. In the playoffs, they did it again. First, they gobbled up six L.A. Raider turnovers and turned them in to 20 points and a 27–20 upset victory. In the AFC title game with Miami, they did it again, grabbing six Dolphin turnovers and winning easily, 31–14. The Pats became the first wild-card playoff team to win three games on the road to get to the Super Bowl. Now it was showdown time with the Bears.

The Patriots were solid both ways. They had young Tony Eason at quarterback with veteran Steve Grogan backing him up. Craig James was an outstanding runner, as was Tony Collins. Irving Fryar and Stanley Morgan represented deep threats, and the offensive line did the job. The defense was opportunistic and able to make its own breaks. While the Bears were solid favorites, there were many who thought the Pats had a good shot at the upset, especially if they kept forcing and retrieving turnovers.

It started well for the Patriots. The Bears had the ball first, but on Walter Payton's second carry, he fumbled and the Pats got the ball at the Chicago 19. "Team Takeaway" was at it again. But three Eason passes went incomplete and New England had to settle for a Tony Franklin 36-yard field goal. The Patriots were ecstatic. They had the lead and had proved the Bears weren't invincible.

Only no one bothered to tell the Bears. They must have thought it was 1940 again, when their counterparts blasted the Washington Redskins, 73–0. Once they got started, nothing seemed to stop them. They drove downfield, propelled by a 43-yard McMahon-to-Willie Gault pass. Kevin Butler kicked a 28-yard field goal to tie the game, allowing the Bears to re-establish themselves.

While the defense was shutting down the Patriot offense, Chicago's Jim McMahon led his team to a great, 46–10, triumph in 1985, the Bears first title since 1963.

Now the defense began to move. Eason tried to throw and was thwarted again and again. Minutes later, a Tony Eason fumble gave Chicago the ball at the Pats 13. The New England defense again prevented a touchdown, but Butler booted a 24-yarder to make the score 6–3 with 1:26 left in the first period.

Another New England fumble once again presented Chicago with the ball at the 13. Two plays later, fullback Matt Suhey rambled 11 yards for the score. The kick made it 13–3 at the end of the first period. Then early in the second period the Bears drove again, this time 59 yards on 10 plays. McMahon took it in from the two, and the kick made it 20–3. The game was getting out of hand in a hurry.

The Pats had already changed quarterbacks. Eason had failed to complete a pass and was shell-shocked by the blitzing Chicago defense. Grogan fared a little better, but on this day nothing was going to stop the Chicago steamroller. A Kevin Butler field goal made it 23–3 at the half. In effect, it was all over. But the Bears weren't through.

They came out for the second half like gangbusters. First, there was a 96-yard drive, highlighted by a 60-yard pass to Gault, with McMahon scoring from the one. It was now 30–3 after the kick. Minutes later, Reggie Phillips intercepted a Grogan pass and ran it 28 yards to the end zone. The kick made it 37–3. And before the period ended, the Refrigerator plunged in from the one to culminate a 37-yard parade. Butler's boot made it 44–3.

The primary target for quarterback McMahon's passes was speedy wide receiver Willie Gault, shown here ready to grab another one for a long gainer, as Patriots defenders close in too late.

The Pats finally got one early in the final session, but it was basically meaningless. A Chicago safety midway through the period ended the scoring, ended it at 46–10. The Monsters of the Midway were back, and back with a bang. As the stats show, they had totally dominated the game.

As the Bears built up a 44–3 lead through two and one half periods, they held the Patriots to zero yards in total offense. At halftime, the Pats had minus 19 yards and they didn't complete a pass or get a first down until five minutes before the half. The Chicago defense intercepted two passes and recovered three fumbles. And a defensive player, end Richard Dent, was the game's Most Valuable Player.

It was a great moment for the Bears and the city of Chicago. The legacy started by George Halas was not forgotten. And while it might have been a great moment, it was also a frightening moment, frightening for all the other teams in the league that might meet these Monsters of the Midway in 1986 and beyond.

Bill Gutman has been an avid sports fan ever since he can remember. A freelance writer for fourteen years, he has done profiles and bios of many of today's sports heroes. Although Mr. Gutman likes all sports, he has written mostly about baseball and football. Currently, he lives in Poughquag, New York, with his wife, two step-children, seven dogs and five birds.